William Thomson

A tour in England and Scotland in 1785

William Thomson

A tour in England and Scotland in 1785

ISBN/EAN: 9783743345447

Manufactured in Europe, USA, Canada, Australia, Japa

Cover: Foto ©ninafisch / pixelio.de

Manufactured and distributed by brebook publishing software (www.brebook.com)

William Thomson

A tour in England and Scotland in 1785

A TOUR

IN

ENGLAND AND SCOTLAND,

IN 1785.

BY AN ENGLISH GENTLEMAN.

LONDON:

PRINTED FOR G. G. J. AND J. ROBINSON,
PATER-NOSTER-ROW.

1788.

Stack Annex

ITINERARY,

WITH THE PRINCIPAL

CONTENTS.

LONDON.		
Miles		Page
58	OXFORD -	3
	Woodſtock	
17	Blenheim *and back*	}
19	Chapel-Houſe	6
	Haythorp -	6
10	Shipſtone -	9
12	Marſtone	
5	Edge Hill	
15	Stratford -	10
10	Birmingham	11
7	Sutton - -	20
9	Litchfield .	21

Miles		Page
12	Burton -	24
12	Derby -	25
16	Matlock -	25
	AND	
8	Environs -	25—29
	Aſhbourn -	29
4	Dove-Dale -	30
12	Bakewell -	30
3	Chatſworth -	30
5	Stoney Middleton	32
12	Buxton -	33
9	Caſtle-ton Peake, &c. - -	} 34
5	Chapel-in-Frith	38
20	Man-	

a

Miles		Page	Miles		Page
20	Manchester	38—42	5	Hawkes-head	54
19	Worsley and back	42--44	6	Conistone	54
			5	Low-Wood	55
25	Warrington	44	20	Bowness *and round the* Windermere Lake	53—56
12	Prescot	45			
8	Liverpool	45—47			
20	Canal, Leeds	47	16	Ditto, ditto	56—58
3	Ormskirk	47	18	Keswick	58
19	Preston	49	10	Skeddaw	60
11	Garstang	49	12	Barrowdale	61
11	Lancaster	49	15	Ulls-Water	64
9	Hornby	50	5	Penrith	67
10	Kirby Lonsdale	51	18	Carlisle	68
12	Kendal	51			
9	Bowness	52		606 *in ENGLAND.*	

SCOTLAND.

Miles		Page
18	ANNAN	70
18	Dumfries	71
21	Moffat	74
14	Elvanfoot	76
	Drumlanrig	77
	The Clyde, *the* Tweed, *and the* Annan	77
14	Douglass-Mill	78
14	Lanerk *and the* Falls *of the* Clyde	80---85
15	Hamilton	

Miles		Page
5 Hamilton	— —	85---87
Bothwell Caftle	— —	88
11 Glafgow	— —	90---99
7 Paifley	— —	95---98
Cruickftone Caftle	— —	100
15 Dumbarton	— —	101
13 Lufs		
Loch Lomond, *with the Southern Afpect of the Highlands*	—	104---111
8 Tarbat	— —	109
Glencroe	— —	112
14 Cairndow	— —	113
10 Inverary *and* Loch Fine, *with a Plan for promoting the Fifheries*	- -	114—123
16 Dalmally, *with Loch-Awe*	- -	124—127
12 Oban, *Bunawe, Loch-Etive, Furnefs-Company, Cruachan, Dunftaffnage, Dunolly, and Appin*	- - -	127—132
18 Glencoe, *King's Houfe, and Tyndrum*		133—135
24 Fort-William, *with the neighbouring Lakes*		135—144
14 Letter-Findlay, *with the adjacent Country*		144---145
14 Fort Auguftus, *with the neighbouring Mountains, Rivers, and Lakes*	- -	145---149
14 General's Hut *and Fall of Foyers*	-	148
11 Invernefs, *with its Environs, and the Soil, Climate, and Contour of the Country*		149---153

Culloden-

Miles		Page
	Culloden-Moor, *Cauder Castle, Fort George,* and	
15	Nairne - - ..	153
12	Elgin, *with* Forres, *and a remarkable Inundation* - - -	154---158
9	Fochabers, Gordon Castle, *and Strictures on the general Mode of planting Trees in Scotland* - - -	158---161
12	Cullen - - -	161
11	Bamff - - -	162
16	New-Deer - - -	164
16	Peterhead, *with the Castle of Slanes, and Boilers of Buchan* - -	164---167
16	Ellan, *with a Seat of the Earl of Aberdeen's*	167
16	Aberdeen - - -	167---172
15	Stonehaven, *with Dunotter Castle* -	172---173
10	Innerbervie - - - -	174
13	Montrose - -	174---176
8	Brechin - - - -	176
12	Forfar, *with Marle-Lakes and Glamis Castle*	176---177
18	Cupar - - -	178
15	Perth, *with a Geographical Description of the central and most celebrated Parts of Scotland* - - -	178---193
	The Improvements *around in Agriculture and Manufactures, and the public Spirit of the Perthshire Gentlemen and others,* -	ib.

Miles		Page
	Scone *described, with the Circumstance that rendered it a fit Place of Residence for the Scottish Kings*	191---193
	Strathern, *the distinguished Beauty and Fertility of that Valley*	193---200
20	Auchterarder, *the Seat of a Presbytery famous for a Mixture of Popish Claims and Antinomian Doctrines—The Druidical Gloom that surrounds it*	201
	The Vale, *with the Falls of the* Devon—*and the antient Castles of the Marquisses of Montrose and Argyll*	202---207
14	Dunblane——*the* Sheriff-muir, *Approach of the* Ochills *to the Grampians---Grazing, and Hints concerning it*	202---209
5	Stirling	210
	Historical Account *of the Royal Palaces in Scotland*	210---213
	Highlanders, *Character of, with various Anecdotes*	214---229
	Feudal System *and Aristocracy in Scotland, the* Revolution, Darien, Union, *and Abolition of Heritable Jurisdictions*	231---246
	Bannockbburn, *Battle of*	246---252
12	Carron, *and* Falkirk	252---256
10	Linlithgow	256

18 Edin-

Miles		Page

18 Edinburgh, *its Situation, Caſtle, Origin of Edinburgh, and of Burghs in general, New Town, public Buildings, Hoſpitals, Character of the Lowland Scots in general, and the Edinburghers in particular, Progreſs of Commerce and Arts, the Univerſity of Edinburgh, Places of Amuſement, and the State of Religion* - 256---342

Saliſbury Craggs *and* Arthur Seat, *with the View from thence* - - 290---294

Leith, *the Sea Port of Edinburgh* - 294---298

Advantages *of lowering in Scotland the Duties on Ale and Beer, and a Commutation Tax propoſed for this purpoſe* - - 304

Murder *of Capt. Porteous, with the Fate of his Aſſaſſins* - - 336---341

12 Burnt-Iſland
12 Edinburgh, *back to*
14 Black Shiels
12 Lawder
16 Sydenham
8 Kelſo
8 Coldſtream

} · · · · · 342---343

769 *in SCOTLAND.*

ENGLAND.

Miles		Page

MILL-FIELD Plain, *with the Battle of
Flouden* - - 344---351
16 Wollerhaugh
18 Alnwick - - 352---354
*This Town, with the whole Coaſt from New-
caſtle to Berwick, admirally fitted for Woollen Manufactures* - - 354
*Sundry Obſervations and Anecdotes concerning
the antient Kingdom of Northumberland,
during the Roman, Saxon, and Norman
Æra* - - 354---360
*A Liſt of Words, the ſame in the Norwegian
and the Icelandic Languages, and in that of
the Lowlands of Scotland, and the Northern
Counties of England* - 360---362
*Hints for rendering the Union between Eng-
land and Scotland more and more complete,
and for ſecuring the Liberty and Proſperity
of both* - - 363---367
16 Wollerhaugh
18 Alnwick
18 Morpeth
15 Newcaſtle
10 Shields
15 Durham

Miles		Miles	
15	Durham	15	Harbro'
18	Darlington	9	Lamport
18	North Allerton	8	Northampton
19	Eafingwould	15	Newport Pagnel
13	York	9	Wooburne
9	Tadcafter	10	Dunftable
14	Leeds	8	St. Alban's
9	Wakefield	11	Barnet
12	Bank Top	12	London
12	Sheffield		
12	Chefterfield	377	
12	Mansfield	606	
15	Nottingham	983 *in ENGLAND*	
14	Loughbro'	769 *in SCOTLAND*	
11	Leicefter	1,752 *Miles*	

DIRECTIONS TO THE BINDER.

The Prints to be placed thus:

1. *Ulls Water*, a Lake in Cumberland, - fronting page 65
2. *Stone Byers Lynn* on the *Clyde*, - - - 81
3. *Bothwell Caftle*, - - - - 89
4. *Town and Caftle* of *Inverary*, - - - 120
5. The *Caldron Lynn*, - - - 205
6. *Edinburgh Caftle*, - - - - 257

A

T O U R

IN

ENGLAND AND SCOTLAND.

....

THERE is not one hour in the life of any man that is exactly the fame with another, during the whole courfe of his exiftence, from the cradle to the grave. New objects, circumftances, and fituations; new ideas, emotions, and paffions, blended together, according to their different fhades and order of fucceffion, and producing fancies, hopes, and fears, in endlefs variety, render human life the moft variegated as well as the moft fleeting fcene with which we are at all acquainted in the whole circle of nature. As the power of language is unable to arreſt and deſcribe the mixed emotions of the mind at the moment they paſs, ſo it is far leſs fitted to recall them at pleaſure. But if we cannot clothe in language, and mark down, the various ſentiments and feelings that occupy our minds in different times and ſituations, it is in our power, in ſome meaſure, to make up for this deficiency, by recording the objects that occaſioned them: and the diaries in which theſe are comprehended, afford, at leaſt to him who takes the trouble of making them, a very curious and intereſting ſubject of both entertainment and improvement. If the unvaried and unintereſting voids of life ſhould ſeem but little adapted to the compoſition of ſuch journals, travels and voyages not only furniſh materials for collections of this kind, but naturally induce men to make them. It was merely with a view to that ſpecies of amuſement which ariſes from the recollection of intereſting ſcenes, and the emotions which they excited at the time when they

paſſed

passed under observation, that the Writer of the following memorandums ever thought of committing them to paper. And it is in the importunity of friends, an apology that ought not by any means to be accounted the less weighty, that it is trite and common, (since nothing is more common than what is agreeable to truth and nature) that he takes shelter from any charge that may be made of vanity and self-importance.

Accompanied by friends, whose social sympathy enlivened the impressions produced by the varying scenes through which we passed, I left Oxford, on the 17h of May, 1785. Oxford and Cambridge may be justly considered not only as venerable monuments of antient times, but as a kind of garrisons established by public authority, for the preservation of loyalty, literature, and religion. If our univerfities may be thought, in some respects, to check and retard the progress of knowledge, by means of fixed forms, laws, and customs, it is at least equally certain, that they are falutary bulwarks againſt the pre-cipitate and defolating fpirit of innvovation. The reverence paid by our anceſtors to piety and to learning, ſtrikes us in Oxford as by a fenfation, and ſhews how fit objects thefe are of eſteem and veneration to the common fenfe of mankind. For different nations, and races of princes and kings, have concurred, in the courfe of many centuries, to pay homage to the ſhrines of faints and the feats of the mufes. It is not an eafy matter to prevent or to ſhake off a refpect for any noble or royal family, whofe antient reprefentatives, the founders and benefactors of the different colleges and halls, are brought to remembrance by pictures, ſtatues, charters, and ſtately edifices. Thefe take faſt hold of the ductile mind of the ſtudents, and are affociated in their memory with many of the moſt pleafing ideas that have ever occupied their minds. From impreſſions of this kind, a love of their early haunts and companions,

naturally

naturally affociated together in the imagination, is nourifhed in the breafts of the noble and generous youth, and alfo an attachment to their king and country. Take away thefe memorials of antiquity, thofe noble and royal teftimonies of refpect to fanctity of life, and proficiency in learning, remove every fenfible object by which fentiments of early friendfhip, loyalty, and patriotifm are kindled and inflamed in young minds, and difperfe our young noblemen and gentlemen in other countries for their education, or even in feparate little academies and fchools in our own, and you weaken one of the great pillars, by which the conftitution and fpirit of England is fupported and perpetuated.

The univerfities, therefore, and the practice which ftill happily prevails, of educating in thofe great and antient feminaries, the Britifh youth of diftinction, are of very great political importance: nor would all the confequences that might accompany or flow from their fubverfion, a matter which has of late been talked of by certain political reformers and other *agitators*, be for the better.

As to letters, although every man may have a master in literature and in philosophy, who is able to retain him, in the same manner that he can provide himself with a drawing or fencing master, yet we are not by any means to overlook the advantages arising from public libraries, a concourse of learned men for guides and companions, and also the use to be made in great universities of the principle of emulation.

The venerable genius of Oxford, inspiring such reflections as these, seemed to hover around us, until we arrived at Chapel-house, a very good inn, where we dined. Visit Haythorp, the residence of the Earl of Shrewsbury, a very good house, elegantly furnished, and pleasantly situated. The ground around it is well laid out, but not very extensive. The avenue to the house, which is upward of a mile long, is formed of of clumps of trees, inclosed by stone walls about five feet in heighth, which in England are called stone hedges, and in Scotland dykes. These fences, if they do not beautify and warm any country so much as living hedge-rows, possess this advantage, that they may be quickly raised, and, by the power of money, almost in an instant. They do not harbour flocks of birds; they may be built where quicksets will not grow, and they take up but little of the ground, whereas a ditch and hedge take up a great deal. Indeed, in soils where stone walls are more easily raised than quickset hedges, it may be readily supposed that land is of no great value. But this will, in many instances, be found a rash conclusion. Every soil may be turned to great profit by skilful agriculture, provided only, that it be dry, as stony ground for the most part is, or may easily be made. Where the land is covered, as it is in many places, with loose and detached stones, the industrious improver gains at once

once a two-fold object : he clears the ground, and collects materials for building fences. It is obſerved that land, gained from overſpreading ſtones, is uncommonly fertile. This fact, which is well authenticated, is highly deſerving of the inveſtigation of chymiſts. I have alſo heard it affirmed, on this ſubject, that in ſome ſoils the land is the moſt fruitful in oats, barley, and other grain, where the expoſure is backward, that is, where it declines from the ſun.

The ſoil in the neighbourhood of Haythorp does not appear to be well calculated for producing large timber. It may, however, be excellently adapted to the production of other kinds of wood, both foreſt and fruit trees. It is common for men of large fortune to endeavour by all means, and at very great expence, to raiſe by a kind of forced culture, both exotic and domeſtic plants. And many adventurous farmers fight againſt nature, in attempting to raiſe wheat, or other valuable crops, in ſoils fitted only for oats or rye,

rye, or at beſt, for peaſe, or a light kind of barley. To know the nature of the ſoil is the firſt thing requiſite in an improver of the ground: and it is by ſtudying this above all other things, that the man of fortune will beſt diſplay his good taſte, and the farmer increaſe his ſtock, and fill his barns.

May 18th. Leave Chapel-houſe, paſs through Long Compton, a very poor village, and dine at Shipſton. The country between and about thoſe places is open, cold, and ill cultivated; the ſoil is a clay, and there are no rivers. Here, it would ſeem, there is at once great need, and great encouragement for planting, which would give genial warmth to the atmoſphere, and, in the courſe of time, convert the various influences of the heavens into a nutritive, vegetable mould, which being mixed with the clay ſoil, could not fail to open and improve it. The trees produced would be of great value, as they would not only be of uſe for building, firing, and the fabrication of various utenſils neceſſary

both

both for the purposes of agriculture and domestic œconomy, but might also be launched by the Avon into the Severn, and so conveyed to sundry harbours and docks for shipbuilding.

In this bleak tract, ill cultivated and thinly inhabited, it is not uncommon for the lowest or labouring class of the people, who find little other employment in the depth of winter than that of threshing out corn, to lie a-bed the greater part of the day as well as the whole night, in order to save fuel, and to spare their scanty provisions.

Sleep at Stratford upon Avon. Some good houses in this town, which is of considerable extent, but in general ill built, and very badly paved. The bridge here, laid across the Avon, consists of fourteen arches, but is very old. The town-hall is a handsome room, in which is a picture of Shakespeare, and another of Garrick, by Gainsborough. Shakespeare's monument in the church does but little credit to the artist.

May

May 19th. Leave Stratford, pass through Henley, a long town; the houses very indifferent. Dine at Oakeley Moor-house, a small but neat inn. The soil here is much better than in the southern parts of Warwickshire; the country better cultivated, and tolerably well wooded. In the evening arrive at Birmingham; but this being unfortunately the time of their fair, we could not see any of the manufacturers at work. Visit Clay's manufactory for making tea-boards, buttons, and other articles pasted together and dried. Visit also Boulton's manufactory for plated articles of all sorts of steel and iron-work. This town is very extensive, and a great part of it elegantly built. It contains upwards of one hundred thousand inhabitants; but the people are all diminutive in size, and sickly in their appearance, from their sedentary employment. In Birmingham there is one very elegant and spacious church, three chapels, and eight meeting-houses for Dissenters. This town is far

from

from being diftinguifhed by zeal in religion. Dr. Prieftly's latitudinarian principles are adopted by thofe who confider themfelves as philofophers; but the great mafs of the people give themfelves very little concern about religious matters, feldom, if ever, going to church, and fpending the Sundays in their ordinary working apparel, in low debauchery. What religion there is in Birmingham is to be found among the Diffenters. It is well known that there are many coiners of falfe money in Birmingham, a circumftance that is eafily accounted for, from the nature of the bufinefs in which they have been accuftomed to be employed. It may be added, that there is a great deal of trick and low cunning among the Birmingham manufacturers in general, though there are, no doubt, fome exceptions, as well as profligacy of manners. This may be owing in part, to their want of early education; for the moment that the children are fit for any kind of labour, inftead of being

fent

sent to school, they are set to some sort of work or other: but it is probably more owing to their being constantly associated together both in their labouring and in their idle hours. It is remarkable, that society corrupts the manners of the vulgar as much as it sharpens their understanding.

About fifty years ago, there were only three principal or leading streets in Birmingham, which at this day is so crouded, and at the same time so extensive a town: a circumstance which illustrates, in a very striking manner, the rapid increase of our manufactures and trade in steel and iron. It is not above three years since pavements or footpaths, formed of flag-stones upon the London plan, were first introduced in this place. The ladies of Birmingham at first considered these smooth pavements as very great grievances. They were not so convenient, they said, as their old foot-paths, or easy to walk on. And this was the more remarkable, that the streets, side-paths, and all, were not laid with

good

good paving, but with round hard ftones about the fize of large apples, and of courfe fuch as appeared to ftrangers to be very troublefome to the walker, and even painful.

The manufacturers of Birmingham who are generally accounted rich, are fuch as poffefs fortunes from five to fifteen thoufand pounds. A few are in poffeffion of much larger capitals : but in general, they may be faid to be in eafy and flourifhing circumftances, rather than very rich or affluent. The number of carriages kept by private perfons has been doubled within thefe ten years : fo alfo has that of the women of the town. Thefe different fpecies of luxury feem to have advanced in proportions pretty nearly equal. The people of Birmingham have often tried to eftablifh a coffee-houfe; but found this impoffible, even with the advantage of a fubfcription. They generally refort to ale-houfes and taverns. According to the fize of the place, there fhould be feveral coffeehoufes, taking our ftandard in this matter,

from

from London. But the genius of Birmingham is not that of coffee-houses; at least, the coffee-houses of this day: though it might be suitable enough to that of those described in the Spectators and Tatlers. The labouring and poor people of Birmingham fare but hardly; their chief sustenance being bread and cheese, and ale for which they pay five-pence the quart, though this measure is not so large as a quart porter-pot. There is a porter brewery at Birmingham, the liquor produced by which is equal in strength to that brewed in London, but far inferior in flavour.

It is not above seventy years since there was any great variety of metal goods fabricated here. Coarse locks and hinges, with common metal buttons and buckles, formed before that period, the whole amount of the Birmingham manufactures. But now, these coarse articles are manufactured in Wolverhampton, Walsal, Dudley, and other small towns near Birmingham. The fine and fashionable fhionable goods are manufactured in the town of Birmingham itfelf. In the country round about are nailers and woodfcrew-makers, who work in their own cottages, and whofe prices are fo low, that they get but very little money by all their labour. The women and children, as well as the men, are employed in the manufacture of thefe articles. Sometimes the whole family will be occupied in one branch of bufinefs, which fuits well enough, as the father of the family makes large nails, and the wife and children fmaller ones, according to their ftrength. This divifion of labour in the fame family, if ftudied and practifed in different kinds of Britifh manufactures, might in this country, as in India, expedite bufinefs, and alfo improve the articles produced by it.

The induftry of the people in thofe parts is wonderful. They live here like the people of Spain and other hot countries, rifing at three or four o'clock in the morning, going

to

to reſt for a few hours at noon, and afterwards working till nine or ten o'clock at night.

It is exceedingly remarkable, and highly worthy of obſervation, that induſtry in manufactures in the diſtricts adjacent to Birmingham, is wholly confined to the barren parts of the country. This great town ſtands on the ſouth-eaſt extremity of a very barren region. On the north and weſt, but chiefly on the north-weſt, where the land is very poor, that is, on the road to Wolverhampton and Shrewſbury, the country is full of the moſt induſtrious manufacturers in the coarſe branches of buſineſs, both in detached houſes, and in villages and ſmall towns, for many miles: but on the other ſide, which is Warwick-ſhire, as you go from Birmingham towards Coventry, Stratford on Avon, and Worceſter, a circle including the points of eaſt and ſouth, and nearly that of weſt, where the ground is fertile and well cultivated, there is ſcarcely a manufacturer to be found of any kind, and in iron and steel none at all; though you come by degrees into the countries where spinning and weaving is carried on, manufactures of a less laborious nature than those of steel and iron. It might be thought at first sight, that the difference in question might be accounted for, from the single circumstance, that it is in the very centre of the barren region that the pits are found, which supply the manufacturers with the essential and encouraging article of coal. But the marked and sudden contrast between the barren and the fertile districts, in respect of application and industry in manufactures, is not fully explained by this circumstance alone, for within two miles of Birmingham, they are on the one hand all farmers, and for twelve miles on the other, they are all manufacturers.

The people of Birmingham, I speak of the middling and ordinary class of manufacturers; retain in many things, as has been already observed in the instance of their attachment to taverns and other public houses, the

man-

manners of other times. They are expenfive in eating and drinking, and in clothes too. But they give themfelves no trouble about the ftile or mode in which they live. Men who employ under them great numbers of workmen, and who fpend from two to three hundred a year, live in their kitchens, which are kept remarkably clean however, in good order, and well furnifhed. This is by no means mentioned as a matter of either contempt or reproach, but the contrary. There is a natural and indeed neceffary connection between induftry and œconomy, as there is between both and the profperity of a nation. From the introduction of luxury and the decay of manufactures, the United Provinces have begun to decline in wealth, population, and power. Indolence and pleafure, the parents of idlenefs and corruption, have begun to fap the foundations of a ftate which was raifed on induftry, temperance, and frugality.

The navigable canal which communicates with the Trent and the Severn, terminates at this town. By this canal Birmingham is fupplied with almoft every article that is wanted, and particularly with coals, which are dug out of pits about eight miles diftant, and which, by this mode of conveyance, are rendered fo cheap, as to be commonly fold for fix fhillings and eight pence per hundred Tun weight. The canal is about thirty feet wide. The boats are feventy feet long and five broad, and will carry twenty-five tons, (the draught of water being about four feet and an half) which the canal will admit of when it is quite full. This boat is towed by a fingle horfe.

May 21ft. Leave Birmingham, and pafs through Sutton, a very neat little town, fituated on an eminence commanding a very pleafant profpect; the country around highly cultivated and tolerably well wooded; and vegetation much more forward than in the more foutherly parts through which we had paffed. There is not perhaps any fpot that can be fixed on more centrical than this to the kingdom of England, and at a greater diftance

from

from the fea. Dine and fpend the evening at Litchfield.

May 22d. Litchfield is a fmall city, well built and pleafantly fituated. The cathedral is fmall but very antient, and remarkable for its three fpires, two of which are at the weft end, and one nearly in the centre. There are no manufactures in this city: but it is the refidence of fome genteel families with middling independent fortunes. This was the birth-place of Dr. Samuel Johnfon, of whom fo much has been faid, that it is but little that can remain for the curiofity of his greateft admirers. I was informed of two fingularities in this great genius, which, I think, have efcaped the refearches of all his biographers. There is a great iron ring fixed by a ftaple in a ftone in the centre of the marketplace, which formerly ferved as a neceffary inftrument in the favage diverfion of bull-baiting. When Johnfon happened, in his walks, (for he paid an annual vifit to Litchfield) to pafs by this fpot, he would frequently, in the midft midst of those reveries in which he seemed to be involved, step aside, and stooping down, lay hold of the ring and pull it about, as if he had been trying whether he was able to extricate it from the stone in which it was fixed. The other remarkable particular concerning Dr. Johnson, which has not been mentioned by his numerous biographers, is, that he made it a point when he made his annual visit to the place of his nativity, to call on every person in that city with whom he had the least acquaintance; but that the instant he knocked at the door, he would without giving time for opening it, pass on to another, where he would do the same thing: so that it frequently happened, that two or three servants would be running after the doctor, requesting that he would return to their masters or mistresses houses, who waited to receive him. The people of Litchfield were long, I avoid speaking in the present time, strongly tinctured with Jacobitism. When the Pretender, at the head of some Highland clans, had marched in 1745 into

into Lancashire, the inhabitants of Litchfield, it is said, waited for his arrival there, in his progress to the capital, with impatience. The profound reverence that Johnson entertained for monarchical principles, and hierarchical establishments, was in perfect conformity, and perhaps originally derived from the genius that predominated in the place of his nativity.

A very singular club is held annually at Litchfield of females only. It consists of an hundred members and upwards; and however extraordinary this meeting may appear, yet it seems to have been established from the best of motives, for I have been informed that a considerable sum of money is annually collected and distributed among the poor of the city. About a mile from Litchfield is Barrow-cope Hill, remarkable for being the burying-place of three Saxon kings who were slain in battle.

May 23d. Leave Litchfield, and dine at Burton upon Trent, which we cross about seven miles

miles from that city at Wichnor-bridge, and a mile further, crofs the navigable canal which goes to Derby. Ride by the fide of this canal, about two miles, to the place where it is carried over the river Dove, upon twelve arches. To one who had never before feen one river carried acrofs another, this appearance naturally feemed extraordinary; but on examining the means, or mechanifm on which it depended, wonder at the effect was loft in the contemplation of the caufe.

Burton is a pleafant well-built town: the church a very neat one. A large cotton-mill is erected here, worked by underfhot wheels: we were not permitted to fee the infide of it. There is a very good bridge at Burton, of very great length. The country between this town and Derby is highly cultivated, well inhabited, and tolerably clothed with wood, though the timber is not large. All this country is remarkably full of thorn-hedges. The town of Derby is much larger than Litchfield, is adorned with many very hand-

handsome houses, and in general well built. It is washed on one side by the river Derwent, on which is a very large silk-mill, I believe, the first which was built in this country. It is wrought by one wheel, of twenty-four feet diameter, which gives action to one hundred thousand movements. This mill we were permitted to examine. Near this complicated machine is the manufactory for china; the elegance, as well as expence of which is well known.

·May 24th. Dine at Derby. Ride to Matlock-bath in the afternoon. About three miles from Derby, the face of the country changes all of a sudden, from a fine fertile vale, well wooded and inhabited, which you leave behind you, to high hills, to the north, which are clothed to their very summits with excellent grafs. The inclosures here are formed entirely of stone, with which the soil abounds, though it is by no means unfertile. At Crumford, about a mile from Matlock, the road is cut through a rock, just wide enough

enough for a carriage to pafs. As foon as you get through this, the view which prefents itfelf is highly curious and romantic. Immediately below runs the river Derwent, bounded on each fide by high and rugged rocks, in fome places perpendicular, in others covered with wood. The ride to Matlock from this pafs, and all the dale, is equally wild and romantic. We took up our quarters at the Old Bath, which is kept by Mr. Mafon, where we found good accommodation. Our landlord behaved with great civility, and was at great pains to fhew us the country all around; but I faw no fpot, in this variegated region, which delighted me fo much, or which appeared fo great an object of curiofity, as the Vale of Matlock itfelf. On the hill, towards the north-weft of the village, are many mines which produce lead, and alfo fome copper and antimony. Some of the fhafts are dug to the amazing depth of one hundred and twenty fathom, each of them being wrought, for the moft

part,

part, by no more than two men, whose profits and advantages are confiderable, when they are fortunate enough to hit on a good vein; and, being admitted as co-partners with the proprietors, they are encouraged to continue their refearches until they find one. During the time of their fearching the ground, for a courfe of metal, they receive only one fhilling a day. Great advantages are granted to thofe adventurers, as they are allowed by law to try for one wherever they choofe, on any man's eftate, gardens only excepted. And, if they are not fuccefsful, the only redrefs the proprietor of the land can have, is the power of compelling the miners to fill up the fhaft again. This is a great inconveniency to the gentlemen refiding in that part of the country. The method of making thofe fhafts, which are not above three feet wide, is, to put diagonal pieces of wood into the fides. Thefe fupport the earth where it is loofe, and at the fame time afford fteps to go down by, as they feldom

make

make ufe of any rope or chain. This bufinefs of mining affords many advantages, and prompts to the ftudy of natural hiftory. The nature and the arrangement of the mineral ftrata, in the mines of Cornwall and Devonfhire, fuggefted their leading ideas to Woodward in his Theory of the Earth, and to Mr. Hutchinfon, who attempted to frame a fyftem of natural philofophy, agreeably to the writings of Mofes. If academies for obfervation and experiments were eftablifhed in the mining countries, philofophy might be advanced thereby with greater rapidity than has yet diftinguifhed her progreffive courfe. Lord Bacon juftly obferves, that if the kings of Egypt had beftowed as great pains and expence in digging holes into the bowels of the earth, as they did in raifing thofe ftupendous moles called pyramids, on its furface, they would have rendered greater fervice to mankind, and acquired to themfelves jufter and more lafting fame. Such pits being dug to their hands by private adventurers, it would be

an

an honour to princes, as well as an acquisition to the general stores of knowledge, to appoint men of science to make observations on the different substances brought to light by the persevering and penetrating industry of miners, in different parts of the world.

At Crumford are two very large cotton mills, the property of Mr. Arkwright, which he was so obliging as to allow us to see. To attempt a description of a piece of mechanism so curious and complicated, would be vain. I can only say, that the whole process of cleaning, carding, combing, twisting and compleating the yarn for the loom, seems to be done almost without human aid. The different machines are prepared for working chiefly by children, of whom Mr. Arkwright employs at this place about one thousand.

27th May. Leave Matlock, and go to Ashbourn by Wirksworth. The road is good, but the country very hilly and dreary. From Ashbourn we proceed to visit Dove-Dale, which is about two miles long. Through this

this dale runs the river Dove; and on each side of it, are many high and barren rocks, which, to a man who has never viewed the rugged face of nature, would appear tremendous. I cannot say that they had any such effect on me. From this dale we went to Bakewell, a very poor ill-built town. The little river Wye runs through Bakewell, and about two miles below, glides through a beautiful meadow, where there is a very old house, called Haddow-Hall. Near this town is another very large cotton mill, belonging to Mr. Arkwright's son, apparently as large as that at Crumford.

Saturday 28th May. Leave Bakewell, and go to the Duke of Devonshire's at Chatsworth. This place, from its situation, seems calculated for a residence of only a few months in the year. The country, about two miles round the house, is well wooded, and by great pains and industry, highly cultivated. But all the distant hills within view of the house, wear a dreary and dismal aspect.

The

The garden or pleasure ground, is confined, and laid out with very little taste: for tho' there be a command of water from a spring on the hill behind the house, a fountain and cascade is exhibited, which, in the midst of summer, must indeed have a pleasant appearance; but the steps over which the water runs being artificial, after having seen it once, you cease to admire it. The house is built of a dark yellow stone, and the west front of it is very elegant. A pretty large quadrangle is formed in the centre, which makes the rooms dull and gloomy. Some of the apartments are spacious and lofty, but ill-furnished, and without any historical picture that is worthy of notice. The river Derwent, which runs through the park, has a pleasing effect, and a bridge, thrown over it, which leads to the house, does great credit to the architect. It consists of three arches, which are truly elegant. Though this house and the garden be situated in a low vale, yet the gardener told us, that it is impossible to

ripen

ripen fruit here, without hot walls. The chapel is very fpacious, as well as elegant. Some of the trees are nine feet in circumference; but thefe are chiefly firs, and have been long planted.

Dine at Stoney Middleton, a very poor village, and ride afterwards to Buxton through Middleton-Dale, which very much refembles Dove-Dale, except that it is not watered, like that valley, by any river. Having paffed through this dale, we afcended a very high hill, which commands a moft extenfive though barren and fullen profpect: not a tree to be feen, and the tops of the hills bare rocks, although the fides of thefe towards their bafes, and the fmall vallies between, are covered with very good verdure. The inclofures in this dreary tract are very fmall, formed of ftones piled up into walls, to clear the land, and to fcreen the cattle. And fuch as this is the whole country around Buxton. This place, from the efficacy of its waters, has grown into a large

ftraggling

straggling village. The houses are chiefly, indeed I may say solely, built for the accommodation of invalids. The Duke of Devonshire has lately built some elegant houses in form of a crescent, which has a very pretty appearance. This building, I was told, would cost the Duke about 50,000l. But I should imagine, he will never get tenants for all those houses, as I can scarcely suppose it possible, that any person would reside at Buxton but from necessity; to receive benefit from the water, which, in all rheumatic cases, is certainly very efficacious. The bath is about the 82d degree of heat, and very pleasant to the feeling of every person that enters it. Near Buxton there is an hill, in the bowels of which several hundred people find daily employment.

Monday, 30th May. Leave Buxton, and go to Castletown, a poor small town, inhabited chiefly by miners. Near to this place is the celebrated cavern called the Devil's A—se, the mouth of which is really tremendous, being fourteen yards in heighth and depth, and ten yards wide. After having advanced to the end of the mouth, you are conducted through a small door, which leads you into the cavern. At 450 yards from the entrance you come to the first water, the roof of the rock gradually sloping till it comes within about two feet of the surface of the stream which passes through the cavern. This water is to be crossed by lying down flat, in a small boat, on some straw. The boat is pushed forward by the guide, until you get through this narrow and low place, which is about four yards long. After landing on the other side, you come to a cavern seventy yards wide and forty yards high, in the top of which are several large openings; though the candles were not sufficient to enable us to see their full extent. Having crossed the water a second time, on the guide's back, you come to a cavern called Roger Rain's house, because from its roof there is a continual dropping of water. At this place you are entertained by a company of fingers, who have taken another path, and afcended to a place called the Chancel, about thirty feet higher than the place on which you ftand; where, with lights in their hands, they fing various fongs. The effect of the whole is very ftriking. The water is, in all, croffed feven times; but you can ftep over it, except at the two firft places. At one place, the ftream is loft in a quick-fand, but emerges again at a great diftance, without the cavern. The whole extent of this extraordinary fubterraneous place, as meafured by Sir Jofeph Banks, is 617 yards, and at the furtheft end, is upwards of 200 yards from the furface of the earth. At this fpot the rock comes down, and clofes with the water, fo as to preclude all farther paffage: but, as there was reafon to believe, from a found that was conftantly heard, that there was a cavern beyond this boundary, a gentleman, about four years ago, was determined to try if he could not dive under the rock, and rife in the cavern, on the other fide. With this defperate refolution he plunged in with his feet foremoft; but, as was expected, ftruck his head againft a rock. In this ftate he remained a confiderable time, till at laft he was dragged out by the hair of the head. About the middle of the old cavern, the man who fhews this place, has found out another paffage, in a different direction, which he calls the New Cavern. Into this we went, with difficulty, about an hundred yards; but the ftones were fo loofe under our feet, and the roof of the cavern, in feveral places, fo low, that we did not choofe to take the trouble of going farther, though the guide fays, that its extent is near 200 yards. This man is fo eager in purfuit of new wonders in this cave, that I fhould not be in the leaft furprifed to hear of his being buried or drowned in it; for in winter, the whole of this fubterraneous place is fometimes full of water, as clearly appears from a great quantity of mud and fand which ftick to the rocks on all fides. It is indeed the paffage of the

the water that has evidently been the cause of this natural curiosity. This has washed away, in the course of time, the mud and sand which filled the cavities of the rocks, and thus scooped those vacant spaces which form the caverns.

If this tremendous cave were properly lighted up, and music placed in different parts, with the witches in Macbeth and their cauldron, and other infernal agents and machines, such as are introduced on the stage, a more wonderful effect might thereby be produced, than has ever resulted from any mimick or natural scene.

Above the mouth of this cavern is the ruin of a very old castle.

On the south side of Castletown stands Man-torr, a very high hill, one side of which appears to be mouldering fast away. On the top of this hill are the remains of a Roman encampment, and near its base is a coal mine. The coals are conveyed in boats, under ground, near a mile, to the bottom of an hill,

hill, and then put into carts. Each of those boats carries about a ton. From Castletown proceed to Chapel-in-Frith, a small neat town: sleep at the George Inn, where there is most excellent accommodation.

Tuesday, 31st May. Leave Chapel-in-Frith, and ride through Whaley and Stockport, to Manchester. After ascending the hill above Whaley, the face of the country assumes a new and more pleasing aspect, being changed from rugged rocks and lofty mountains, to fertile vales and beautiful woods. The whole country, for a great many miles round Manchester, is exceedingly well cultivated, and fertile. This town is old, and of large extent; and in the skirts of it, you are struck with the appearance of many elegant houses. But, on the whole, it is not so large, or so well built as Birmingham. The road from Stockport to Manchester, a stretch of nine miles, is paved.

Wednesday, 1st June---*Manchester.* Notwithstanding what I have said of the town of Manchester, the industry in the manufactures carried on here and in the neighbourhood, cannot fail to excite the most agreeable emotions in the minds of all Britons. And, if it be inferior to Birmingham in respect of extent, and of building, it is superior to it in point of police or internal regulation, and also in the stile or mode of living. The population of this great town is not less than 75,000. There are not so many people of middling fortunes as in Birmingham, but there are more persons who have great fortunes: a circumstance which is to be accounted for, from the nature of the Manchester manufactures, which cannot be so well carried on as those of Birmingham, by tradesmen of small capitals. The manufacturers of Manchester live like men of fortune, which indeed they are.

The greatest part of the people are engaged in some useful art, but principally in finishing the goods that are manufactured in the neighbourhood. The mills, which I have before

before mentioned, prepare the cotton for the weavers, and Manchester completes the work. From hence the goods are carried to every part of the world; the conveyance of these being greatly facilitated by the communication which the canals afford with the sea, on either side of the island.

Manchester is the best regulated town in England, though, like Birmingham, it is not governed by magistrates of its own, or a town-council, but by the gentlemen of the town, who are at great pains to establish order and good manners among the lower people, by good regulations. The people, again, being mostly weavers, and consequently, orderly and domestic, are very tractable, and susceptible of good government. The work-house here pays better, I believe, than any in England. The poor inhabitants earn, on an average, four pence a day, though in many others they scarcely gain a farthing.

The streets are paraded every Sunday, during the time of divine service, by constables, who

who take all straggling persons into custody. Disorderly houses are searched once in every eight or ten days, about nine or ten o'clock in the evening, care being taken not to let it be known when the search is to be made. And, as all this is done not by trading justices, and other fellows in office, but by gentlemen, it answers the purpose of preserving order, without bustle, expence, or oppression.

The spirit of enterprize is extended, in Manchester, from manufactures and commerce to mechanical invention, and from thence to philosophy in general. They have, in this exemplary community, a philosophical society, who pursue literature and science with all the ardour that is natural to new establishments; and also a music room, and regular concerts, ornaments of which no other manufacturing town in England can boast. When the manufacturers of this kingdom were in danger of suffering by the Irish propositions, the town of Manchester took the lead in opposing them, and contributed

buted twice as much as all the kingdom befides, to the fupport of the manufacturers who efpoufed their caufe. It is remarkable, that in this elegant and well regulated town, the inns are the moft inconvenient, incommodious, and in all refpects the worft that can be well imagined. The hotel is indeed better, though not by any means very good : nor will it at all ferve the purpofe of travellers who ftop on their journey only for a fhort time. The women of Manchefter, and indeed of all Lancafhire, are efteemed handfome, and in this refpect, the title of witches may be beftowed on them without great impropriety.

Thurfday, the 2d of June. Go to Worfley in the Duke of Bridgewater's paffage-boat, by his canal, which has been of fo great fervice to Manchefter, and all the adjacent country : the diftance ten miles. At Worfley is the mouth of the funnel which leads to the Duke's coal mines. This funnel, which is five feet high, and fix feet broad,

goes

goes two miles under ground. At one thousand yards from the entrance, a shaft is dug to clear the mine from foul air. Several of those shafts are dug at various distances, for the same purpose. This mode of giving vent to the foul air, has been found necessary, as many fatal accidents have happened from the damp air, and sometimes explosions which have destroyed many of the people who wrought in those mines. I could have wished to enter this subterraneous passage myself, but was told that there were no people at work, and that the air was so foul, that it would be too dangerous. The boats which go through this subterraneous navigation, are of two sizes : the smallest, two and an half feet wide, and twenty feet long ; the largest, five feet broad, and fifty feet long, carrying about twenty-five tons of coal. The miners receive from twenty pence to three shillings a day, according to the quantity of coals they dig, and they work only eight hours. I am told that 250 tons of

coals

coals are brought out in a day; and that above 300 men are constantly employed in this business. After the coals come through this subterraneous passage, they are carried to Manchester and other towns, in the same boats. Sometimes they are put into larger ones, and conveyed to all parts of the country; to Warrington, to Runcorn, and, by the Mersey to Liverpool.

Return to Manchester by the canal, in the same boat, which carries at least sixty passengers, and is perfectly commodious and convenient, having two cabbins in it, for the accommodation of different classes of people; and it is so well regulated by the Duke, that no improper company can go in it, as he has given orders to the boat-master to return them their money, and to set them on shore, provided any of the passengers are guilty of improper conduct.

Friday, the 3d of June. Leave Manchester, and go by the Duke of Bridgewater's canal twenty-five miles, to Warrington.

This

This canal is very wide, and capable of conveying boats of five feet draught of water. Thefe boats are about fixty feet long, and ten feet broad. Sleep at Warrington, a large and well built town. The principal manufacture carried on here, is that of canvafs. The original maker of crofs-bows firft refided in this town, and the fame bufinefs is ftill carried on by fome of his family.

Saturday, the 4th of June. Leave Warrington, and go to *Liverpool*, through Prefcott, a neat little town, commanding a beautiful view of a very rich and well cultivated country. This profpect is bounded on the fouth-weft by the Welch mountains, which appear very high and rugged. Liverpool is a town well known for its maritime enterprize and extenfive commerce. The old part of the town is ill built, and the ftreets rather narrow. Great additions have been lately made to it, and many elegant houfes

are

are erected in its neighbourhood. Here are fourteen building yards, and three of the most commodious and complete basons for receiving ships I ever saw. These basons are capable of holding near 400 vessels, from 500 tons downwards; and can, if necessary, receive any ship, as there is twenty feet water at the dock gates. Here are also two dry basons at low water, by which the ships enter from the river, and go into the inner basons, where they are constantly kept a-float, and can be completely laden, and go to sea without anchoring in the river. These basons are surrounded with excellent ware-houses, and spacious keys for landing the goods. In short, I will venture to assert, that Liverpool is the most complete commercial sea-port in Great Britain. All the works just mentioned have been completed by the Corporation, who are very rich; and, I make no doubt, considering its extensive commerce, but they have an ample interest

for

for the money they have fo laudably expended.

The Duke of Bridgewater has a dock and ware-houfe here, where the veffels which come through his canal are repaired. In Liverpool there are five churches, and about 70,000 inhabitants. The Duke of Richmond has erected a fort at the weft end of the town, which appears to be an ufelefs profufion of the public money; for the entrance into the river is fo intricate, that it is almoft impoffible for the enemy to annoy the town. On the eaft fide of Liverpool is a terrace, commanding a delightful view of the town, the river, and all the neighbouring country. This place is called the Mount, where there is a very good inn.

Monday, the 6th of June. Leave Liverpool, and go to *Ormſkirk*, by the Wigan canal, a diftance about twenty-five miles. Several boats are kept on this canal for the convenience of paffengers, but they are by
no

no means fo well regulated as the boats on the Duke's canal; for we were witneffes of much diforder, and very improper conduct, which muft make thofe vehicles very unpleafant to females. This canal muft have been made at much lefs expence than the Duke's, as the country through which it paffes is very level, and not interfected by any confiderable rivers. The bridges are made of wood, and turn on a centre, by means of a circular iron, and iron wheels. Thefe bridges are conftantly out of repair, and are attended with confiderable expence. The Wigan canal was intended to have been carried to Leeds; and accordingly, the country was furveyed, and the level traced for this purpofe. But an hill, near Whatley, I am told, is an infurmountable obftacle to the accomplifhment of this project. This canal, I have been informed, does not, at prefent, return upwards of two per cent. to the proprietors. The chief article that is carried on it, is coals.

From

From Ormſkirk go in a poſt chaiſe to Preſton: the country between which places is low and ſandy. This tract affords not any ſtriking proſpect; but it is well cultivated, and appears to be good grazing ground. Preſton is a very old town, ſituated on an eminence, commanding a pleaſing proſpect all around it, but more particularly from that point from whence you view the ſeat of Sir Harry Houghton, on the banks of the river Ribble, which winds prettily round the eminence on which it is ſituated, and the diſtant hills in the weſt craven of Yorkſhire bound the view.

Tueſday, the 7th of June. Leave Preſton, and go on to Garſtang. The road between theſe places is exceedingly good; the country well cultivated; much paſture land, but little corn; and no timber, all the trees being cut off by the weſterly winds. Dine at Lancaſter, an old and ill built town, and the ſtreets very narrow. The caſtle, which is ſituated on an eminence that commands the town,

town, was built by Agricola; and, though it bears all the marks of antiquity, yet seems to be in a perfect state. This is now the county jail, which we visited, and were happy to find the prisoners well lodged, and kept clean. Lancaster has been a place of considerable trade, but seems now on the decline. The view from the castle is very extensive, but by no means pleasant.

Wednesday, the 8th of June. Sleep at Hornby. About three miles from Lancaster, enter the vale of Lonsdale, which is very beautiful. On the right is a barren ridge of mountains: in the middle runs the river Loon, through rich and fertile meadows; and on the left the hills are covered with hanging wood; the whole forming a most delightful and charming view. The village of Hornby is small, and the houses are very indifferent. Near the town is a very old castle, belonging to Mr. Charteris, from whence there is a most beautiful prospect of three rivers, the vale, and distant barren mountains.

The

The caſtle is now uninhabited, and falling to ruin. Leave Hornby, and ride by the ſide of the river Loon, to Kirby-Lonſdale, the moſt picturefqe, perhaps, and delightful ride in Britain. Kirby-Lonſdale is a neat, well built little town, ſituated on an eminence; and the river Loon runs cloſe beneath it, through a rich and well cultivatd vale. The adjacent and lower hills are finely covered with wood; and behind theſe, high and craggy mountains are preſented to our view, deſtitute of trees, and of every kind of vegetation or verdure. The contraſt between the bold and barren rocks, on the one hand, and the verdant woods and luxuriant vale, on the other, heightens the rude majeſty of the former, improves the ſwelling ſoftneſs, and the richneſs of the latter, and on the whole, forms the moſt delightful view I ever beheld.

Thurſday, June 9th. From Kirby-Lonſdale proceed to Kendal, ſituated on the river Ken, a town of conſiderable extent and of great antiquity. A great number of people are employed here in the manufactures of cotton and woollen cloths, a great part of which is carried to Liverpool, from whence it is exported to the Weft Indies and to Guinea. This town abounds with tanners.

To the north-eaft of Kendal, on an high eminence, which, in the fouthern and eaftern parts of England, would be called an hill, are the ruins of a very old caftle, with a deep ditch around it, of a circular form, and very fpacious within; its diameter being near 150 yards. Three bridges are built over the river. The low land in the neighbourhood of Kendal is fertile, but it is furrounded by barren mountains and craggy rocks.

Leave Kendal, and pafs through a country, than which one more barren, hilly, and dreary, cannot be imagined. Ride to Bownefs. About a mile from this place we difmount from our horfes, and afcend an hill covered with rude and craggy rocks, which

com-

commands a view that exceeds all defcription. From this point is feen the greater part of the Windermere Lake, and ten iflands. On the largeft of thefe there is an houfe, built in a circular form, at prefent belonging to a Mr. Chriftian, who purchafed both ifland and houfe for 1,700l. This ifland is not only beautiful in itfelf, from a variety of grounds, and clumps of trees, but it is fo happily fituated as to command a view of many of the enchanting objects on this lake. The other iflands are much fmaller than this, but have a charming effect from being richly adorned with wood. The margin of this lake is furrounded with rich meadows, fertile hills, and beautiful woods, with perpendicular precipices, and old yews and hollies growing out of the fiffures of the craggy rocks; all of them fo curioufly mixed and interfperfed, and reflecting their images fo accurately and fo clearly in the tranfparent expanfe below, that it would be difficult to conceive how nature herfelf could form a more captivating fcene.

From different points of view, thofe natural beauties fhew themfelves in different fhapes. Some of the ableft pens have been employed, and the imagination of the poet has been racked, to give a defcription of this beautiful difplay of nature; but language is unable to convey the emotions that this fcene excites, even with the aid of the moft faithful pencil. Therefore, whoever wifhes to have a juft conception of Windermere Lake, and its furrounding beauties, muft view them on the fpot.

Friday, June 10th. Crofs the ferry from Bownefs, and walk to Hawks-head, about four miles diftant. This village is fituated at the upper end of Eftwait-Water, which is about two miles in length, and half a mile broad, furrounded with fine woods and fertile meadows. At the upper end of this piece of water is a good houfe, called Belmount, commanding a view of the whole. In the afternoon we went to the head of Conifton Lake, but a thick fog coming on fud-suddenly, we were deprived of the pleasure of seeing it, and obliged to return to Bowness by Ambleside and Low-wood Inn: but the same fog which prevented us from seeing Conniston Lake, hindered us also from seeing the adjacent country.

Saturday, June 11th. Leave Bowness, and ride to the south end of Windermere. The road is exceedingly good, and carried within a quarter of a mile of the lake, from one end to the other, sometimes through delightful woods, where, for a short time, the water and surrounding hills are hid from your view; but the water and opposite shore now and then appearing, as you advance, through the trees. Sometimes you ride over fertile and beautiful vales, and frequently under high mountains, whose cliffs hang over the road. There is not any part of this ride, which is continued for fourteen miles, that is not highly picturesque, and fitted to afford the most soothing ideas and exquisite gratification.

Return by Bownefs, and go to Low-wood Inn to dinner. This inn is fituated about two miles from the north end of the lake, clofe upon its banks, and commands a profpect of all the upper part of the lake, and as far down as Windermere Ifland, with feveral of the fmaller iflands around it. But from this point they are fhut in with the furrounding head-lands, and lofe their infular appearance, by which the beauty of the profpect is confiderably diminifhed.

Sunday, June 12th. Having met with a difappointment in our attempt to fee Conifton Lake on Friday, and being determined to have a view of all the beauties which this extraordinary country affords, we ride to Conifton in the morning, which is at a diftance, from Low-wood Inn, of nine miles. The road is not very good, but the furrounding fcenery is fo interefting, that we had but little time to look down. After riding about feven miles, we got to the top of an hill, from whence Conifton Lake is

to

to be feen in its full extent. It is a beautiful fheet of water, furrounded by rich meadows. The lower parts of the adjacent mountains are well covered with wood. There is, however, by no means fuch variety in the fcenery here as in Windermere, The hills affume a more regular appearance in their fummits, and reach, in general, to the water's edge in a more gentle defcent. The want of iflands, too, is a great deficiency. Conifton Lake fhould be feen before Windermere, as it certainly has great beauties, though by a comparifon with Windermere, they are confiderably leffened. The north end of Conifton Lake is very bold and ftriking: and here we admire the fituation of Conifton-Hall, on an eminence, and furrounded with fine hanging woods, with rich pafture land below, reaching to the edge of the lake. Behind and above the hall, feveral mountains rife with tremendous majefty, craggy, bleak, and barren; from the bofom of one of which a cataract iffues, which, in

wet

wet weather, muft add confiderably to the grandeur of the fcene.

Return to Low-wood to dinner, and in the evening walk to the upper end of Windermere. About two miles up in this romantic vale, is a houfe belonging to Sir Michael Le Fleming, called Rydal-Hall. In this vale runs the river Rothay, winding through beautiful woods and verdant meadows, till it falls into the lake. On each fide of the river are ftupendous, black, and barren rocks. Clofe by Rydal houfe is a water-fall, where Sir Michael Le Fleming has built a fmall houfe, in a moft fequeftered and convenient fpot for enjoying it. The fall is indeed nothing extraordinary, as it does not exceed twelve feet: but the noife of the water, and the dark fhade of the trees around, form a gloomy fcene, which fills the mind with a pleafing melancholy.

Monday, June 13th. Leave Low-wood Inn, and ride through Amblefide to Kefwick, a fmall village, at the head of Windermere Water,

Water. Paſs by Sir Michael Le Fleming's ſeat; and, at the diſtance of a quarter of a mile, enjoy a charming view of Rydal-Water, in which are ſeveral beautiful iſlands! A little further on is Rydal-Paſs, from which you look down upon a ſmall lake, called Graſsmere, in a moſt fertile vale, ſurrounded by mountains. A few miles from hence is Thirlmere, or Thirl-Water, a delightful lake, extending through a vale about four miles long. Near the middle of this lake, a promontory extends from each ſide, and confines the water to the ſize of a ſmall river, over which is a ruſtick bridge. Aſcend an high hill, from whence there is a moſt tremendous view of a deep and diſmal glen, through which we paſſed, and aſcended another mountain, where the eye is delighted with the enchanting view of Keſwick-Vale, the noble lake of Derwent-Water, and part of Baſſenthwaite. This vale in circumference includes about twenty miles, and the land is exceedingly fertile.

Dine

Dine at Keswick, a neat little town, situated at the north end of the lake. The afternoon was spent in rowing about upon this beautiful sheet of water, which is three miles long, and one and an half wide. Four islands, called Pocklington's, Lord's, St. Herbert's, and Rapsholm, add greatly to the beauty of this water. Some are covered with verdant turf; others are planted with various trees. On Pocklington's Island is an elegant modern-built house, the ground about which is laid out with much taste. After having viewed the magnificent prospects around this lake, from different stations, the rugged and perpendicular rocks of Barrowdale, and the verdant bosom of Skiddaw, return to our inn at Keswick, and

On Tuesday the 14th, ride to the top of Skiddaw, which I believe is computed to be about 1,000 or 1,100 yards perpendicular from Derwent-Water. This mountain is by no means difficult of access, and is covered with grass, which gradually grows coarser

as

as you afcend, till you come within a quarter of a mile of its fummit, where it is very fteep, and where the atmofphere is fo rarified, as to prevent vegetation. The whole top of the mountain is covered with a loofe brown flaty ftone, upon which it is difficult to walk. On reaching the fummit, we were deprived of having the view we expected, of the furrounding country, which in clear weather muft be very extenfive; but unfortunately at this time, all the diftant objects were obfcured by a thick haze. Return to Kefwick.

Wednefday, the 15th. Go in a boat to the upper or fouth part of the lake, and vifit the romantic regions of Barrowdale, where there is fuch a mixture of tremendous and beautiful fcenery, as perhaps no other fpot on earth can exhibit. To defcribe the component parts which form the wonderful whole, would require the genius of Thomfon or Salvator Rofa.

In this vale is a remarkable mine, where an abundance of mineral earth, or hard fhining

ning ftone, is found, which we call black lead, and which is fold for ten fhillings per pound. This is faid to be the only mine of the fame kind in Europe. It is opened once in five or feven years, and a fufficient quantity taken out to anfwer all the purpofes to which it is applied for that period of time.

Through the vale winds the River Derwent, which forms the lake, and afterwards paffes into Baffenthwaite-Water. After having fpent the morning in this delightful vale, return to an houfe called Low-dore Inn, which is fituated clofe by a celebrated fall of water, called by the fame name. The cataract falls from a vaft heighth, through a large chafm, from one craggy precipice to another, until it is loft in the lake. After heavy falls of rain, this natural exhibition muft be tremendous. Return in the evening, with reluctance, to Kefwick.

After viewing this elyfium, which affords the greateft gratification to every traveller, we could not avoid indulging one melancholy

choly reflection---that the defcendants of the antient proprietors fhould ftill be deprived of their birth-right. The liberality of the Britifh parliament has been nobly exercifed, in returning the forfeited eftates in Scotland. It is to be hoped, that the fame benevolence will be extended to the family of Radcliff.

Thurfday, June 16th. We ride to Ulls-Water, at the diftance of fifteen miles, a great part of the way over a dreary moor, and the country round very barren. In this moor we were caught by a violent hail ftorm. Being entirely expofed, we were obliged to turn our horfes backs to the ftorm, and to ftand ftill till it paffed over; for the hail-ftones were fo large, that it was impoffible to face it. Dine at Pulobridge, a very bad inn, where we could not get any beds. Go on five miles, and fleep at Penrith.

On Friday 17th, return to Ulls-Water. Ride on the fide of the lake, five miles, to Lyulph's Tower, an houfe lately built by Lord Surrey, (now Duke of Norfolk) in form

form of a caftle, for the accommodation of his friends, and thofe who go to fee the lake. The conftruction of this houfe is very whimfical. It has two circular turrets. In the centre, which is flat, is an enormous window, which ferves to light feveral rooms within the turrets, which are large enough for bed-rooms. The outfide of the building is quite in the ftile of an old caftle; and viewed from the water, has a very pretty effect. Leave our horfes at Lyulph's Tower, and go to the upper end of the lake in a boat. Return to the tower to dinner, which was a very decent one, and recommended by a very kind reception. After dinner, walk about a mile from the tower, up a dale, where there is a cafcade. This fall is much fuperior to any that I have feen in this country, being fifty feet, and having a greater body of water in it.

Ulls-Water is fixty fathom deep, and in many places very fteep. It is about ten miles long, and nearly three miles broad, and has

Uls. Water: A Lake in Cumberland.

has more the appearance of a lake than any of the others, as you can look over, at one view, a greater expanse of water. Like the others, it is surrounded by high mountains and perpendicular rocks; and, in many places, are yews, holly, and birch, apparently growing out of the solid mass of stone: some young, and in a flourishing condition; others worn out with age. On the banks of the lake there is a great deal of pasture, and some arable land. There are several good houses here, situated so as to command most beautiful views. The land also round the lake is well wooded. But in general, Ulls-Water is by no means so well adorned with wood as the other lakes, particularly Windermere. At the upper end, however, there is a remarkably fine wood, reaching from the water's edge nearly to the summit of the mountain, which is, at least, one thousand feet high. This wood consists of holly, birch, yew, and oak; and though none of the trees are large, it neverthelefs makes a beautiful appearance. At this end of the lake there are three little iflands, or rather rocks, covered only with a few fhrubs; and at the fartheft extremity is a little village, called Patterdale, furrounded by fine wood and rich meadows. A river runs through this village, which falls into the lake. In an old ruinous houfe there lives a mifer, who calls himfelf the King of Patterdale.

In the evening we return by water, to the fouth end of the lake, which is adorned by a beautiful hill, belonging to Mr. Haffel, called Dunmallet. This hill is covered with a variety of trees, and the different fhades of green have a pleafing effect. Sleep at Penrith. Between this place and Ulls-Water, the country is well cultivated, and enriched by feveral gentlemen's feats, with large plantations about them; among which are the antient feats of the Earl of Surrey and Lord Lonfdale: the former called Grey-Stock Park, the latter Lowther-Hall.

Satur-

Saturday, 18th June. Penrith is a neat well built little town. On an eminence are the remains of an old caftle. The church is a very handfome and fpacious building. In the church-yard there are two very remarkable ftones, about eight feet high, and fifteen feet afunder, with three very curious ones between, put edgeways, and joined at the top. This, I fuppofe, has been the burying place of fome antient warrior; but the antiquarians have not been able to decypher the infcription, or to trace the antiquity of the monument. On an high hill, to the north of the town, ftands a watch-tower, or beacon, built entirely of ftone, which commands a very diftant view of all the country round, and was formerly intended to give the alarm of the approach of an enemy. To the north-eaft is a range of very high mountains, called Crofs Fells, or the Britifh Alps, on which the fnow, in large quantities, is very vifible. In fome places, I am told, it remains all the year round. Dine at Penrith,

and

and ride to Carlifle in the evening. The country between thefe two towns is very capable of cultivation, and actually undergoing rapid improvement. In this tract of country, there is much corn land; and, about Carlifle, there is a great extent of rich grazing land, on both fides of the river Eden, which runs by the town.

Sunday, 19th June. Carlifle is a city of confiderable extent, furrounded by a wall thirty feet high, which is going faft to decay. At the north end of the town ftands the caftle, the rudeft heap of ftones that were ever piled together by the induftry of man. There are four old invalids who take care of the ammunition kept in it, of which there is a confiderable quantity, and 500 ftand of arms. On the walls are mounted thirty guns, from fix to twenty-four pounders, and among thefe the guns with which the town was reduced in 1745, by the Duke of Cumberland. The ditch around the

caftle

castle is a filthy stagnated pool. Between the old citadel or castle, and the walls and mote by which it is separated from the town, is a declining bank, on which there is a row of trees, planted by the hands of the unfortunate Mary Queen of Scots, when a prisoner in Carlisle. There are many very good houses in this town, though, in general, it is very ill built, and excessively dirty, from the circumstances of its being surrounded by a wall, and having only a few outlets. Over the river, which is pretty large, are thrown two very elegant bridges. The cathedral is an handsome old building, in the Gothic style; the stone of a brick-dust red, like the cathedral of Litchfield. Near this edifice there is a very modern church, which looks on the outside more like a ball-room than a place of worship.

Dine at Carlisle, and in the afternoon, crossing the sands at the upper end of Solway Firth, enter Scotland, and pass on to Annan,

Annan, which is distant from Carlisle eighteen miles.

The land between the Solway Sands and Annan, is very poor, being chiefly a black gravel, and bog, producing nothing but heath. The country here is for many miles low and flat, but the road exceedingly good. The town of Annan is small, but very neat. It is situated on an eminence above the river of that name, which winds prettily through the meadows below the town. These, near the banks of the river, produce good grass. Immediately on crossing the Solway Firth, we found the children, and even many of the men and women, without either shoes or stockings. The cottages are miserable huts, made of mud, intermixed sometimes with round stones, (such as are found in the beds of rivers, and as you meet with in tracts that have, in the lapse of time, suffered the influence and agency of water) and covered with turf.

Sleep

sleep at Annan, where there are two very good inns, particularly the Queenſberry Arms; and after dinner,

On Monday, the 20th June, ride in the afternoon, eighteen miles, to Dumfries. On the road from Annan to this place, as from the Solway Sands to Annan, the cottages are built of mud, and covered with turf or thatch, the pooreſt habitations that can be imagined, and extremely dirty. The inhabitants are turned yellow with the ſmoke of the turf, which is their only fuel. A ſimilar effect, I have been informed, is produced, by the ſame cauſe, on the inhabitants of North Holland. The connection between climate, ſoil, food, vegetable effluvia, and other phyſical cauſes, and the complexions or colours of man, and other animals, is for the moſt part as myſterious as it is various; but here it is abundantly manifeſt. Till you come within two miles of Dumfries, the land is ſo exceedingly bad, that it muſt baffle every effort towards cultivation. It ſeems to pro-

produce nothing but peat, which is cut here, in large quantities, and supplies all the country round. Dumfries is a pretty large town, and very clean. It is situated in a low vale. The lands about it are tolerably well cultivated. About three miles from it there is a small house of the Duke of Queensberry's, with some large plantations of fir, which appear to thrive extremely well.

Tuesday, 21st June. Leave Dumfries in the morning; pass Lord Hopetoun's house, around which we find some tolerable woods; but the adjacent country is very barren. The farm houses are in general miserable huts, the people very poor, and the lower class of females exceedingly dirty. The old women, frightful enough of themselves, are rendered still more so by their dress, the outer garment being a long dirty cloak, reaching down to the ground, and the hood drawn over their heads, and most of them without shoes and stockings. Others among them wear what they call *huggers*, that is, stockings

ings with the feet either worn away by long and hard service, or cut from them on purpose: so that the leg is covered by these uncouth teguments, while the foot, that bears the burden, and is exposed to brakes and stones, is left absolutely bare. In the winter, especially in the highland and mountainous parts of Scotland, which include extensive regions on its southern borders, the old women and men very generally wear a kind of boots or hose formed of a coarse thick woollen cloth, or serge, which they call *plaiding*, and which they roll in folds, one above another, for the sake of heat. In the Low Country of Scotland, there are many districts, where the old men yet wear around their loins leathern belts or girdles, fastened by an iron or brass buckle, which, as we learn from sculpture and painting, so late as towards the end of the last century, were very commonly worn even by the Scottish gentlemen. Near Lord Hopetoun's is a remarkable arch thrown over a

deep

deep glen, a very rapid river precipitating itself about sixty feet beneath, through large rocks, which, in winter, cannot fail to make a tremendous appearance. Between Dumfries and Moffat, a space of twenty-one miles, there is not an house in which you can find any accommodation that is tolerable.

Dine at Moffat, a very small town, with some tolerable houses in it, which are let to invalids who come to this place for the benefit of the water. Here are two springs, one of them the strongest mineral in Britain, and of a very bracing quality. It is about four miles from the town. The other, which is of a milder nature, and now commonly used, is about a mile distant, and issues out of a rock about thirty feet high, by the side of a deep glen, at the bottom of which there runs a strong stream. The former spring has been greatly injured by the admission of another stream into it, which has deprived it of two thirds of its qualities.

Moffat

Moffat is furrounded by high hills, and watered by the river Annan, here only a fmall ftream. The land, except that near the tops of the hills, feems very capable of cultivation, and, fuch as by induftry, might produce good corn ; for, wherever an attempt has been made, it feems to have been attended with fuccefs : but their chief attention, in this part of the country, is beftowed on the rearing of fheep, which is done with lefs trouble, and with greater certainty of profit or fuccefs. But, I fhould think, that the culture of grain and the breeding of fheep might be happily united; and that the land in thefe parts might be made more profitable, than it is in its prefent ftate, both to the landlord and tenant, by enclofing the lower parts of the hills, and screening them from the rudenefs of the climate by trees. For in this barren tract, there is fcarcely a tree or wood of any kind to be feen, except a plantation of firs to the north of the town, which are yet in their infancy, but which clearly prove that trees will grow, if the in-

habitants

habitants will only take the trouble to plant them. There is a good house here, belonging to Lord Hopetoun; and the next best is the inn, where there is good accommodation, and an ordinary, as at Matlock and Buxton.

Wednesday, 22d June. Leave Moffat, and ascend an hill, which is nearly three miles in height. From this height you have a most extensive and dreary prospect of the West Highlands, without so much as one single tree or shrub to be seen, which ever way you turn your eye, for thirty miles around.

Ride fifteen miles to Elvan-foot, with this dreary waste on every side. Cross a bridge over the River Clyde, and arrive at a miserable cottage, called an inn, where, notwithstanding its appearance, we got a tolerable dinner, and some very good wine. There is an house here, belonging to Mr. Irvine, which is falling fast to ruin. This inn, and a blacksmith's shop, are the only habitations

to

to be feen in all this country, except a few temporary fhepherds huts. This place may fuit the tranfient purpofes of a traveller, on a fine fummer's day, which this happened to be; but in winter, it cannot be better defcribed than by the following lines:

> Wou'd Heaven, to punifh fome abandon'd wretch,
> Pufh the dread vengeance to its utmoft ftretch,
> Let him, in cold October's wintry ftorm,
> Where fullen heaths the fulky hills deform,
> To bleak *Drumlanrig* * on an hack repair,
> Delug'd with floods of rain, and fhelter there;
> Or fhould this curfed doom be too fevere,
> Let the vile mifcreant find a refuge here.

Among thefe mountains, and only two or three miles from each other, the Annan, the Clyde, and the Tweed, the principal rivers in the fouth of Scotland, derive their fource. Moft of the mountains are covered, even to their fummits, with tolerable grafs. But they feed nothing upon them but fheep, and thefe, by no means in proportion to the extent

---

* The Duke of Queenfberry's feat.

tent of the country. The proprietors of land in the North and Weſt Highlands of Scotland have of late converted large tracts to the rearing of ſheep, that had in all former times been given up to the breed of black cattle. It is for the land-holders and tenants in the South Highlands of Scotland to conſider, whether it would not be for their intereſt, in like manner, to employ certain portions of their paſture lands, in the breed of horned cattle, eſpecially as they have a great advantage over the farmers of the north and the weſt parts of the country, in their vicinity to England. At Elvan-foot is an handſome bridge over the Clyde.

In the afternoon ride to Douglas-Mill, through the ſame kind of wild country, fourteen miles. At this place there is a tolerable inn. About two miles from Douglas-Mill, ſtands the antient Caſtle of Douglas, ſituated on a ſmall river of the ſame name. Of the old caſtle there remains only part of one turret. Near the ſame ſpot there is a new caſtle,

castle, which, however, is not completely finished. This, I suppose, was intended to be like the old one; but three turrets only, and part of the body of the castle, is all that is completed. Many of the rooms are spacious and lofty, but not well executed. The turrets are circular, and have handsome rooms in them, on each story, which, in the upper story, are very convenient, being converted to the purpose of dressing-rooms for the bed-chambers. If this house, or castle, were finished, it would be a magnificent building: but I do not find that Mr. Douglas ever intends to live in it. The park, which is nearly three miles round, is well well planted, and many of the trees are very old. But all the country around, far and near, is open, and, for the most part, nothing but sheep-ground. About a mile from the castle is the village of Douglas.

Thursday, June 23d. Leave Douglas-Mill, and go to Lanerk. Having travelled

about

about three miles, we fall in with the Clyde, the banks of which are under tolerable cultivation, and in some places prettily adorned with hanging woods. In this ride, the country improves every mile, and begins to be enriched by several gentlemen's seats, with plantations about them, which, after the wide wastes and dreary solitudes lately traversed, affords a pleasing relief to the eye, and wears the appearance of comfort. On the right hand, about five miles from Lanerk, is a seat of Lord Hyndford. A mile further, cross a very elegant bridge, of five arches, over the Clyde. Nearly two miles from Lanerk, we get out of the chaise, and walk about a mile out of the road, to an house called Corra Lynn,* belonging to Sir John Lockhart Ross; close by which are the Falls

* It is to this scene that Allan Ramsay alludes, as to the greatest possible hyperbole, when, in his Elegy on John Cowper, a burlesque poem, he says,

O! could my tears like Clyde down rin,
And make a noise like Corra Lynn.

Falls of the Clyde, which exhibit the firſt ſcene of this kind in Great Britain. Many circumſtances concur to render theſe ſublime falls beautifully picturesque: woody banks, the romantic face of the country, and the form of the rocks over which they daſh, ſo varied, as to give the aweful torrent the grandeſt, as well as the moſt diverſified appearance. At the Corra Lynn, the river, which is very large, is precipitated over a ſolid rock, not leſs than 100 feet; and, at Stone-Byers, about a mile higher up the Clyde, there is another fall, of about ſixty feet, where the river, confined within a narrow bed, makes one entire ſhoot over the rock. At both theſe places, this great body of water, ruſhing with horrid fury, ſeems to threaten deſtruction to the ſolid rocks that enrage it by their reſiſtance. It boils up from the caverns which itſelf has formed, as if it were vomited out of the infernal regions. The horrid and inceſſant din with which this is accompanied, unnerves and overcomes the

F   heart.

heart. In vain you look for ceffation or reft to this troubled fcene. Day after day, and year after year, it continues its furious courfe; and every moment feems as if wearied nature were going to general wreck.

At the diftance of about a mile from this aweful fcene, you fee a thick fmoke afcending to Heaven over the ftately woods. As you advance you hear a fullen noife, which, foon after, almoft ftuns your ears. Doubling, as you proceed, a tuft of wood, you are ftruck at once with the aweful fcene which fuddenly burfts upon your aftonifhed fight. Your organs of perception are hurried along, and partake of the turbulence of the roaring waters. The powers of recollection remain fufpended, for a time, by this fudden fhock; and it is not till after a confiderable time, that you are enabled to contemplate the fublime horrors of this majeftic fcene.

It is a certain truth, that fuch falls of water as thefe, exhibit grander and more interefting fcenes than even any of thofe out-

rageous

rageous appearances that are formed by storms, when unresisted by rocks or land, in the troubled ocean. In the sea, water rolls heavily on water, without offering to our view any appearance of *inherent* impetuosity: we desiderate the contrast of the rocky shores, and there is not any such horrid noise.

The cascade at the Corra Lynn, though it falls from the greatest altitude, and in one uninterrupted sheet, is narrow in proportion to its height: that at Stone-Byers, though not much more than half the height of the other, has somewhat in it of greater grandeur. It is three times as wide; its mass is more diversified; its eddies more turbulent and outrageous; and, without being divided into such a number of parts as might take any thing from its sublimity, it exhibits a variety of forms that give a greater appearance both of quantity and of disorder.

In the Corra Lynn, just where the water begins to fall down the horrid deep, there stands on a pointed rock a ruined castle,
which

which about fifty years ago was inhabited. In floods, the rock and caſtle ſhake in ſuch a manner as to ſpill water in a glaſs. Imagination can ſcarcely conceive a ſituation more awefully romantic, or, before the uſe of gunpowder, more impregnable. Sir John Lockhart Roſs has an houſe on the verge of this matchleſs ſcene.

On the edge alſo of this ſtupendous fall of water, ſtands a mill, whoſe feeble wheel ſeems ready to be daſhed in pieces, even by the ſkirts of its foam.

The walk between the higher and the lower falls, is extremely beautiful and romantic. The rocks, on each ſide of the river, are an hundred feet high, and covered with wood. It runs alſo over a bed of ſolid rock, in many places broken, and worn into large cavities by the violence of the water, which, from a variety of interruptions, aſſumes a variety of directions, and in other places forms numberleſs inferior caſcades. The two principal falls, when the river is full,

full, are tremendous beyond defcription. In the fummer months, the quantity of water which it contains, is not generally fo great as to prevent the curious traveller from making fo near an approach, as may enable him to take a minute and accurate furvey of its beauties.

From the Corra Lynn the Clyde continues to run for feveral miles, between high rocks covered with wood; and on either fide are feveral good houfes, very pleafantly fituated, and the land about them well improved. We dined at Lanerk, which is delightfully fituated on the brow of an hill above the Clyde, which commands a very pleafing profpect. Lanerk is a borough town, but fmall and ill built; and the inhabitants appear to be rather in a ftate of poverty. In the evening go to Hamilton, a neat well-built town, with fome very good houfes in it. The inn here, where we flept, is a very good one. It is kept by a Mr. Clarke, from London. At the end of this town is the Duke of Hamilton's houſe, which forms three ſides of a quadrangle, placed in a very low ſituation. Some of the rooms in it are large and ſpacious, but in general, not well furniſhed. Among the pictures which adorn this place, there is one which is indeed capital, namely, Daniel in the Den of Lions. On a hill in front of the houſe, is a fanciful building in the ſtile of a caſtle, where there are two or three ſitting rooms, which command a very pleaſant proſpect. The reſt of the building is allotted to ſervants, and other purpoſes. Here the Ducheſs has a very pleaſant flower-garden, and notwithſtanding the height of the ſpot, every thing in it was very forward at this time, and all the flowers of the ſeaſon in full bloom. From this building is a delightful ride of eight miles, on the verge of a fine wood, which hangs over the River Clyde. In a part of this ride we paſſed by a number of oaks, of much greater antiquity than any we had ſeen ſince we entered Scotland. Near theſe

these venerable trees, and on the top of a rock which hangs over the river, are the ruins of the old castle of the Hamiltons. Of this structure little now remains, except the gateway. Here we were shewn some of the original cattle of the country, lineally descended from the wild ones, but which, like their present masters, have now grown tame and civilized. At the Duke's house is a most excellent garden of seven acres, well stocked The walls are covered with fruit trees, which are in a very flourishing state, and which exhibit not any symptoms of the bad climate complained of in this country. Cherries and strawberries were at this time quite ripe; and most other fruits were brought to maturity, in their proper season, without the aid of art, which was not the case at the Duke of Devonshire's, in Derbyshire. At the Duke of Hamilton's there is also a good hot-house and green-house.

Saturday, the 25th of June. Leave Hamilton, and proceed to Glasgow, a very pleafant ride, through a well improved country, of eleven miles, part of it on the banks of the Clyde. About three miles from Hamilton is Bothwell-Bridge, where a famous battle was fought in 1651, between the Loyalists and Scotch Covenanters. About two miles from this is Bothwell Castle, belonging to the Douglas family, which is a great antient tower, exactly in the stile, as well as corresponding in magnitude, to the old Welch castles. The walls of this large structure, a great part of which is still standing, were sixty feet high, and fifteen thick. This enormous mass, in one part, crushed its foundation, and rock and castle, in one place, fell down together in the Clyde. This breach in the foundation was afterwards filled up, and the wall that had fallen rebuilt. This castle formed an oblong square, or internal quadrangle, with a round turret at each corner, three of which are still entire; but all the internal part is demolished. In the centre of the building stood the citadel,

or

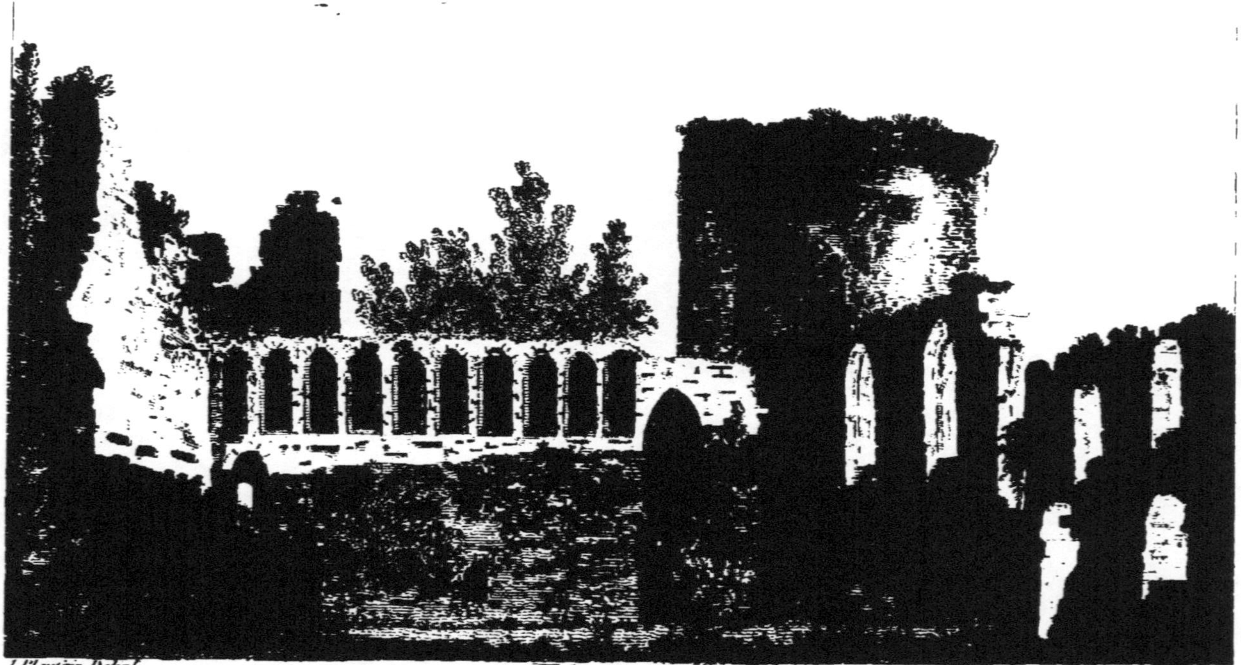

J. Playfair Delin.t Heath sculp.

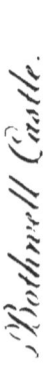

Bothwell Castle.

or keep, which was the moſt inacceſſible part of the caſtle. The windows were placed very high, the bottoms of them being at leaſt fifteen feet from the ground ; and all of them looked into the ſquare, or area. The elevated ſituation of the windows, as well as their internal aſpect towards the great court, were precautions, we may preſume, againſt the arrows or other miſſile weapons which might be thrown into them by an enemy. On the ſame principle we may account for the elevated poſition, as well as the narrowneſs of the windows, in all other antient edifices. On the oppoſite ſide of the river, are to be ſeen the remains of the beautiful Caſtle of Blantyre, belonging to the nobleman of that name. Between this monaſtery and Bothwell-Caſtle, there was a ſecret and ſubterraneous communication, below the bed of the Clyde : ſo that the antient Douglaſſes were ſecured by the architecture, and the religion of the times, as well as the valour of their arms. Near this Mr. Douglas has lately

built

built a very commodious as well as elegant house, in the modern ſtile, on a ſite that commands a view of both the Clyde and the old caſtle.

Dine at Glaſgow, a large and well built city, containing about 50,000 inhabitants. A conſiderable trade has been carried on here, in tobacco and rum, from the Weſt Indies and Virginia; but it is now conſiderably diminiſhed. The capitals, however, the mercantile habits, and the adventurous ſpirit of the people are ſtriking with ſucceſs into new paths of induſtry. The cotton manufactures, particularly, are increaſing here daily, and eſpecially thoſe of nankeens, which are of as good a fabric as thoſe of China.

The college of Glaſgow is about the ſize of the ſmalleſt at Oxford, and is capable of admitting a conſiderable number of ſtudents, although only eight or ten live in it, the reſt being diſperſed in private lodgings in the city. There are professors here, of all the ſciences, many of whom, as Simſon, Hutchinſon, Smith,

Muir,

Muir, Millar, and Reid, are celebrated in the republic of letters. The difperfion of the ftudents in private quarters, here as at Edinburgh, prevents that monaftic difcipline which is ftill preferved, in fome degree, in the two other Scottifh univerfities of inferior renown. But, to balance this difadvantage, if it be a difadvantage, in Edinburgh and Glafgow, the faculties have ftill fome regard to decency, and to the name and dignity of their refpective univerfities, in granting literary degrees.

The principal of the college of Glafgow enjoys an annual falary of 500l. The other profeffors have from 2 to 300; but the profeffor of divinity has nothing; though he is always provided for by fome other confiftent and collateral office, either in the church or univerfity, or both. In the other Scotch univerfities, fmall falaries are allowed to the profeffors of divinity, as well as houfes and gardens: but, then, they are not permitted,
like

like the profeſſors of literature and philoſophy, to take any fees from their pupils; which, according to the nice and delicate feelings of the Scottiſh reformers, would be a ſpecies of *ſimony*, or felling the Holy Ghoſt for money.

The college garden is pleaſant, though not very extenſive. The library, which is a tolerable room, contains about 3,000 volumes.

In the city of Glaſgow there are eleven kirks, beſides ſundry conventicles and meeting houſes. The Eighty-five Societies, or fellowſhip-meetings of the handicraftſmen of Glaſgow, and chiefly the weavers, in which they inſtruct one another in metapyſical notions in theology, are celebrated by the petitions preſented to parliament by Lord G. Gordon. In ſuch, and ſo extenſive a city, lying in the ſouth-weſt quarter of Scotland, it is not to be wondered, that there is not a little grimace and hypocriſy. It is not many years ſince the magiſtrates of Glaſgow, humouring the auſterity of certain of their clergy, and

the

the general prejudices of the people, were wont to be very rigid in enforcing a judaical obfervance of the fabbath. The elders, a clafs of men in Scotland that feem to unite in their perfons fomewhat of the authority of curates, conftables, and church-wardens, ufed to fearch, on the Sunday evenings, the public houfes; and if any perfon, not belonging to the family, was found there, he was fubjected to a fine, or, if he could not give an account of himfelf, perhaps to imprifonment. Yet means were found by all who had a mind to evade the laws of fobriety in the following manner. They called at an elder's houfe, on pretence of feeking the benefit of his prayers or family worfhip. This duty being over, the elder put up his bible on an adjoining fhelf, and took down a bowl, in which he made a fmall quantity of punch, prefenting, at the fame time, fomething to eat, as ham, oat-cake, cheefe, dried fifh, &c. which they call a *relifh*. The elder's bowl being foon exhaufted, each of the guefts, in his turn,

infifted

infifted alfo on having his bowl; for which demands the landlord took care, before hand, to be well provided with rum and other ingredients, which he retailed, in this private manner, chiding his guefts, (at the fame time that he drank glafs for glafs) for their intemperance. The company parted at a late hour, fufficiently replenifhed, it muft be owned, with the fpirit.—

A more liberal fpirit, it is juftice to obferve, begins to prevail here, as in other parts of Scotland. In Glafgow, we find the moft complete abbey that is in Scotland, in which there are now three places for public devotion; one of them in the fpot which was formerly appointed for the burial of the dead; a moft gloomy place, and well adapted to the genius of the Prefbyterian religion. Two handfome bridges extend over the Clyde. In this city, there are two glafshoufes; one for making black, the other for making white glafs. There is a canal from this place to the eaft fea, which will admit

of

of vessels of 150 tons; but the expence has been greater than the commerce * repays, for 500l. shares are now selling for 200l. Had this canal been made only half as large, it would have answered much better.

Sunday, 26th June. Go from Glasgow to Paisley. This town contains 20,000 inhabitants, the greatest part of whom are employed in the manufacture of silk and thread gauze. This last is made from five-pence halfpenny to nine-pence per yard, and the silk from nine-pence to twelve shillings. The people are paid by the yard, in proportion to the fineness of the gauze. Some of the men and women earn five shillings a day for the fine gauze. Very young girls are employed in weaving the coarser sort. Some of them weave three yards a day or more, and can earn thirteen or fourteen pence. Young children are also made useful in preparing the

the

---

* Since writing the above, commerce has been very much increased, and the price of shares in the canal increased, of course, in proportion.

the filk and thread for the loom, and are paid from four-pence to fix-pence a day.

At this place are the remains of an antient abbey, built in the year 1100, part of which is in tolerable order, and ferves inftead of a kirk. There are two other regular kirks in Paifley, and five Diffenting meetinghoufes. The manufactory here was eftablifhed about twenty-five years ago, by an Englifhman of the name of Philips; and it is now increafed to the amazing magnitude of giving employment and fubfiftence to 15,000 fouls. They have lately introduced the cotton manufacture here, which is increafing very faft.

The town of Paifley is near two miles long, and the new part of it, which has been built within thefe five years, contains many very good houfes, built of free-ftone. The principal manufacturers are fixteen in number, feven Englifh and nine Scotch. Many of thefe have made confiderable fortunes, fet up their carriages, and built, in the neighbourhood of the town, elegant country houfes.

Many

Many houses in Paisley pay, in wages to journeymen weavers, women and children, 500l. a week. The carriage of new gauze patterns from London to this place, by the coach and waggons, costs 500l. a year. A fertile country, cheap labour, a sober and steady people, abundance of coal and water carriage, were the circumstances which invited English manufacturers to settle in this country; and the justness of their views has been fully evinced by the most prosperous success.

In the abbey, which belongs to Lord Abercorn, there is a monument of the wife of Robert Bruce, who broke her neck near this place, when she was big with child. The infant was preserved, and afterwards created Lord Semple, and was grandfather to James I. The bells were taken out of this abbey, and are now at Durham. There is a most excellent inn at Paisley, built by Lord Abercorn, and kept in very good order by the present landlord, Mr. Watts, who provided us with a handsome carriage, and horses that performed a journey of 600 miles through the most

G   moun-

mountainous part of Scotland with the greatest ease. The civility and attention of Mr. Watts merits this remembrance.

Monday at Paisley.

Tuesday, 28th June. Return to Glasgow, the country between which and Paisley is pretty well cultivated, and presents several pleasant prospects. The country round Glasgow produces but little corn, nor is there such attention shewn to AGRICULTURE as might be expected near the second city in Scotland. A great deal of ground is appropriated to the purpose of raising vegetables for the table, but they will not take the trouble to water any of the plants, let the season be never so dry. In the city of Glasgow, there are many houses, to all outward appearance, exceedingly elegant. They are, however, only half finished. The window-shutters and doors are unpainted deal, and many of the walls bare plaister. So large and opulent a city as this might have water conveyed into it, and be drained, without oppressing the inhabitants, by which means it would

would be much cleaner, and of course, more healthful. The police of the city seems to be well attended to. It is governed by a provost and twelve inferior magistrates, who take cognizance of small offences, and chastise petty offenders by slight punishments. Two of the justiciary lords come here twice a year from Edinburgh, to try offences of an higher nature, and to inflict proportionable punishments.

The inn, or rather the hotel at Glasgow, called the Tontine, is a very large house. The coffee-room, and ball-room, are very elegant: but there are only six bed-rooms. The liquors, of all kinds, are exceedingly good.

Wednesday, 29th June. Leave Glasgow, and ride to Dunbarton, fourteen miles, on the banks of the Clyde. Many good houses on each side of the road, and both sides of the river well improved and wooded. The Clyde, after passing Glasgow, has level, green, and fertile banks, always filled up to the brim by the rains that fall so plentifully on the western shores of Scotland. Mr. Spears, a merchant in Glasgow, has built near Renfrew,

frew, a very handsome villa, such as a capital merchant in London might have erected on the Thames, at an expence not less than 10,000l.

On the beautiful River Cart, which discharges itself in the Clyde, near Renfrew, about two miles from Paisley, there is a very pleasing seat, belonging to the Earl of Glasgow. The city of Glasgow, and the town of Paisley, ARE BOTH within view of this charming residence. The River Cart meanders sweetly through the park; and Cruickstone-Castle, now in ruins, standing on a most beautiful eminence, adds an interest to the delightful scene, having been a *maison de plaisance* to the unfortunate Mary Queen of Scots. It was here that she indulged her loves with Lord Darnley, during the happy period of their union, and here springs fresh, to this hour, her favourite yew-tree, which she often impressed on her copper coin. The remains of a ditch are still to be traced round the castle, and the ruins are picturesque,

though

though not extensive. In examining the interior parts of this old mansion, you can still distinguish the lofty hall where the tender Mary, among a race of barbarian and ruffian lords, displayed the refinements of France, and the charms of Venus. You can also trace her favourite apartment, where she dedicated the soft hours of her retirement to the loves and graces.

Lady Glasgow, much to her praise, has lately contributed to the preservation of this interesting ruin, by a well-timed support to its decaying foundations.

Dunbarton is a small town, in a semi-circular form, on the banks of the Clyde. Being well situated for receiving kelp from the western coast of Scotland, it has two glass-houses, both of which find full employment. The castle is situated on a rocky hill, nearly conical, rising out of a plain, to the height of 500 feet, defended, where it is accessible, by a wall, and its base washed by the Clyde and the Leven, whose pure stream

flows

flows entirely from Loch-Lomond. The rock of this hill has, at different times, tumbled down in large fragments, which remain upon the plain below, forming an huge mafs of ruins. The country around is for feveral miles quite level. The view from Dunbarton-Caftle up and down the Clyde, is very pleafant, and particularly beautified by the towns of Greenock and Port-Glafgow, which run out into the river. The refidence of Lord Semple, with another feat acquired by marriage, on the fouth fide of the Clyde, and Lord Blantyre's, near Port-Glafgow, are very good houfes, and add to the beauty of this ftriking landfcape. The land about them is well wooded, and greatly improved. The Clyde, above Port-Glafgow, becomes very fhallow, and will not admit of veffels above 80 tons. To the north of Dunbarton, there is a fine vale, well cultivated and peopled; and Ben-Lomond, a very high and ftupendous mountain, forms the back ground of this magnificent profpect.

On

On the castle of Dunbarton are mounted thirty guns. The garrison consists of a captain, a lieutenant, an ensign, and sixty privates. On the south side of the rock there is a good house for the governor. The gunner's house and barracks are higher up, and the magazine, which is bomb-proof, is on the very summit. This bold eminence is not of easy access, at any place, and, if fortified in the modern stile, would be as impregnable on the side of the water as the rock of Gibraltar. It has the advantage of several good springs in it, which produce a sufficient quantity of water for any number of men.

At Dunbarton there is a tolerable inn, kept by Macfarlane, at the Macfarlane Arms. The prison, opposite to this house, forms not a very pleasant object. This day was kept sacred on account of the preparation for the sacrament. At least 1,200 people attended this solemnity; all of them with shoes and stockings, and otherwise very clean, and well dressed. The weather was at this time remarkably hot. The thermometer stood 84.

Thursday, 30th June. Leave Dunbarton, and go to Lufs. The banks of the Leven, up to Loch-Lomond, are fertile and populous. The pure stream is well adapted to bleaching, and other useful purposes. These pleasing scenes, in the fore ground, are contrasted with the purply-blue hills of the Highlands behind, rising over them in aweful grandeur; and the majestic Ben-Lomond, like the father of the mountains, which seem to do him homage, rearing his venerable head into the clouds. And here the traveller from the Low Countries, is suddenly and forcibly struck with the character of the Highlands. The number of the mountains, their approximation to one another, their abrupt and perpendicular elevation: all these circumstances taken together, give an idea of a country *consisting* of mountains without intermission, formed by nature into an impregnable fortress. This is the fortress, which has enabled

the

the natural hardinefs and valour of the antient Caledonians to tranfmit, from the earlieft records of their hiftory, the dignity of an unconquered and independent nation, to their lateft pofterity.

The woody banks of Loch-Lomond, with its irregular form, and its numerous and variegated iflands, running up, and vanifhing at an immenfe diftance, among the bafes of lofty mountains, form an object both aweful and pleafing, and happily unite the beautiful with the fublime.

About two miles from Dunbarton, is a pillar, erected to the memory of Smollet, who was born in this country, on the banks of the Leven, four miles from Dunbarton. Arrive at the edge of Loch-Lomond: go into a boat, and row fix miles to Lufs, which is a fmall village.

Friday, July 1ft. Go upon the lake, in a boat, and dine upon an ifland, called Inchconachan: catch fome good trout, and return in the evening to Lufs.

Saturday,

Saturday, July 2d. Navigate the lake, and go round moſt of the iſlands. A hard gale of wind, and the lake greatly agitated. At Luſs there is a tolerable inn, kept by one Grant.

Sunday, 3d July. Go to the top of an hill, which took two hours to aſcend it, and two to come down. From hence we had a moſt extenſive view to the ſouth and eaſt of Stirling and Edinburgh, with the parts adjacent, and, to the weſt and north of the ſea, and the tops of near an hundred craggy mountains, diſmal, bleak, and barren.

Loch-Lomond is twenty-four miles long, and about eight broad. Near the ſouth end, it has from 20 to 140 fathom water. It is chiefly towards this end, too, that it is interſperſed with various iſlands, to the number of twenty-four. Several of theſe are from one to three miles broad : ſome riſe a conſiderable height above the water, and are well covered with wood : others are flat, and have a great deal of grazing land, and, in
ſome

some places, produce good corn: a few of them are barren rocks, with here and there some straggling shrubs and trees. The southern part of the lake is environed with high mountains. Some of these, sloping gradually down to the water's edge, produce, towards their base, a great quantity of grass, and some corn; particularly, on the south-east side of the loch, where the Duke of Montrose has an house, and much cultivated land around it. On the west side, on a large promontory, well covered with wood, Sir James Colquhoun has built a very handsome modern house, which is beautifully situated, and commands several fine views of the loch. All the northern parts of this great body of water is encompassed by stupendous, barren mountains, rising almost perpendicularly from the transparent surface, which reflects and softens their rude image; with the exception of only a few spots, in which there is a considerable quantity of wood, with some pretty large trees, and in some places a small extent of level ground, which enables the

poor

poor inhabitants to scratch out a few acres of corn and potatoes for their scanty meal in the winter. On the southern point of an island, in this extensive and beautiful lake, called Inchmerran, there stands an antient castle belonging to the Duke of Lennox.

The south end of Loch-Lomond, beautifully interspersed with isles, presents a number of charming prospects: but all the northern part of it, being narrow, and bounded, and overshadowed by the most tremendous precipices, tends only to fill the mind with horror, and leads us to lament the unhappy lot of those whose destiny it is to live within its confines. Very different from this are the lakes of Cumberland and Westmoreland, where an appearance of plenty gladdens the sympathetic heart, as much as the romantic prospects which they afford, amuse the imagination.

On the sides of the mountains that environ Loch-Lomond, near the edge of the water, there is a good deal of birch, oak, and

other

other underwood, with some tolerable trees. This underwood is cut down at the end of every fifteen years. The bark of the oak is peeled off for tanners: and the wood of this, and other underwood and trees, being turned into charcoal, is sent to Glasgow: a species of commerce which must be tolerably productive, as the conveyance from the Loch to the Clyde is all by water. This circumstance tends to stimulate general industry, and to increase the value of the whole vicinity of Loch-Lomond. The fish in this lake are, trout, salmon, perch, pike, &c. which the surrounding inhabitants, notwithstanding the incitement of water conveyance to the Firth of the Clyde, take for their own use only. At the south end of the loch a number of black cattle are fed, and, at the north, a few straggling sheep.

Monday, July 4th. Leave Luss, and ride, by the side of Loch-Lomond, eight miles, to Tarbat, where there is an inn much better and cleaner than that at Luss. Opposite to this inn appears the majesty of Ben-Lomond.

We

We waited two days for an opportunity of ascending it, but the clouds were so low, that it was uncovered but once the whole of this time, and that only for a few minutes.

On BEN-LOMOND.

Stranger, if o'er this pane of glass, perchance,
Thy roving eye should cast a casual glance,
If taste for grandeur and the dread sublime
Prompt thee *Ben-Lomond*'s fearful height to climb,
Here gaze attentive; nor with scorn refuse,
The friendly rhymings of a tavern muse.
For thee that muse this rude inscription plann'd,
Prompted for thee her humble poet's hand.
Heed thou the Poet, he thy steps shall lead
Safe o'er yon towering hill's aspiring head;
Attentive, then, to this informing lay,
Read how he dictates, as he points the way:
Trust not at first a quick advent'rous pace,
Six miles its top points gradual from the base.
Up the high rise with panting haste I pass'd,
And gain'd the long laborious steep at last.
More prudent thou, when once you pass the deep,
With measur'd pace, and slow, ascend the lengthen'd steep,
Oft stay thy steps, oft taste the cordial drop,
And rest, O rest, long, long, upon the top.
There hail the breezes, nor with toilsome haste
Down the rough slope thy precious vigour waste.

So shall thy wondering sight at once survey
Vales, lakes, woods, mountains, islands, rocks, and sea;
Huge hills that heap'd in crouded order stand,
Stretch'd o'er the northern, and the western land;
Vast lumpy groups, while *Ben*, who often shrouds
His loftier summit in a veil of clouds,
High o'er the rest displays superior state,
In proud pre-eminence sublimely great.
One side all aweful to the gazing eye,
Presents a steep three hundred fathom high.
The scene tremendous, shocks the startled sense,
With all the pomp of dread magnificence:
All these, and more, shalt thou transported see,
And own a faithful monitor in me.*

Leave Tarbat, and ride two miles to the top of Loch-Long: an arm of the sea, where the tide rises about six feet. At the north-east end of this loch is a small house, with some firs about it, the residence of the Laird of Macfarlane, renowned, among other good qualities, for his knowledge of Scottish antiquities, particularly genealogies, and for taste and proficiency in the antient Scottish music.

* These lines are written on a pane of glass, at the inn of Tarbat; and they are subscribed J. R.

mufic. Ride two miles round the end of Loch-Long, where there is another houfe of the fame fort, belonging to a gentleman of the name of Campbell, which has a view of Glencroe, with a river multiplied by a thoufand cafcades from the tops of craggy mountains roaring over loofe ftones, juft by his houfe, and difcharging itfelf into the lake. At this place enter Glencroe, which is fix miles long, and at feveral places fo narrow, that the road has been made by blowing out the folid rock, and is carried above the river, which runs over large rocks below, and occupies the bottom of the glen. The fides of the mountains on each hand, formed of black, craggy rocks, are almoft perpendicular. While we paffed through the narrow glen between them, a thick fog rendered this gloomy avenue, at all times aweful, now ftill more dreadful. At the end of Glencroe there is an hill which terminates it, on the fummit of which is a ftone, with the following infcription: "Reft and be thankful."

This

This road was made by the 23d regiment, and cost them not a little labour to accomplish it. From thence, I suppose, arose the inscription; for to the traveller, and even to a carriage, it is neither long nor difficult. From the point of this hill you look down on a small lake, passing by the side of which you enter into another glen, which is much wider at the bottom, and from the edges or extremities of which, the mountains rise with a gradual slope, and afford very good pasture for sheep. This glen reaches by an extent of four miles, all the way to Cairndow, a small village on the north-east side of Loch-Fine, which, like Loch-Long, is an arm of the sea, where the tide rises about six feet. Near this place is a house, belonging to Sir James Campbell, of Ardkinlafs, with a tolerable plantation about it. Dine at Cairndow, a very indifferent inn, and, in the afternoon, pass on, round the north end of the loch, to Inverary. This is a ride of eleven miles, and very pleasant, the road, which runs along the side of the loch, being very good, and the adjacent mountains being well covered with wood.

Inverary and *Loch-Fine*. In Loch-Fine there are no islands. The mountains on each side are so very high, that they are in general covered with clouds. At their basis, near the water, there is a good deal of coppice-wood; and, in some spots, the land is flat enough to admit of corn, and grass for hay. There is a great quantity of sea-weed thrown on the beach, which makes good manure, and is applied to that purpose. By these means, good crops are produced; but so much rain falls, that the poor cottager seldom reaps the fruits of his labour in good condition. The culture of potatoes here, as in every part of the country, is an object of great care and attention, and answers very well. But the corn, after it is sown, is greatly neglected, and suffered to be choaked up with weeds.

This arm of the sea produces herrings in great abundance, cod, haddocks, whitings, and

and various other kinds of fish. Five hundred boats are employed in the proper season for fishing, and are, for the most part, so fortunate as to take a considerable quantity of herrings; part of which are salted for the use of the neighbouring country, and part sent to Glasgow for exportation. This fishing might certainly be increased, and become a source of great profit to individuals, as well as general advantage to the nation.

Whoever has travelled over the western part of Scotland, and viewed the various lochs, and arms of the sea, must naturally reflect on the great advantages which the inhabitants, and the nation at large, may derive from a wise and liberal encouragement to promote the increase of the fisheries on that coast, and more especially when it is considered, that thousands of the natives of that country have very little employment. While my mind was impressed with those ideas, the following plan struck me as the most feasible, being the most likely to encourage industry, and to be attended with the least expence.

Let application be made to Government for a certain number of old fifty gun ſhips, or let any other large and commodious ſhips (ſuch as old Eaſt-Indiamen) be purchaſed, which they may be for a ſmall ſum of money, and let them be ſent round, and moored in ſafe ſituations in the different lochs.

Let Government have the controul of thoſe ſhips, by placing ſome intelligent maſters of men of war, or other officers to command them, with ten or fifteen ſeamen, accuſtomed to fiſhing, in each of them.

The ſhips to be jury rigged: that is, to have ſmaller maſts, yards, and rigging, than would be required for actual ſervice. The rigging of the veſſels is propoſed for the purpoſe of exerciſing the young men who chuſe to engage in the fiſhery, in the practical art of ſeamanſhip.

The young men who chuſe thus to engage, ſhall make theſe their habitations for a certain time of the year, and be ſubject to the orders of the maſters of the ſhips.

A certain number of boats and nets to be found by the society, who are to support the undertaking.

Four skilful fishermen, and four boys, to be employed in each boat.

The boys to be bound apprentices to the society for a certain number of years.

After the expiration of their apprenticeship, the society, or Government, to provide a boat with nets, for every six young men.

And from this time the boat to be considered as their own, for the benefit of themselves and families.

A bounty to be given in proportion to the quantity of fish which each boat takes.

Each ship to have one hundred or more apprentices, to be found in cloaths, bedding, and provisions, by the society, until their time of apprenticeship expires.

The fish to be salted on board the ships, or in any convenient spot on the adjacent shore; and kept on board till vessels arrive to carry them to the different markets.

An emulation between the fishing vessels would be heightened, if different ships were manned,

manned, and drew their apprentices from different clans: and, that the whole might be cheered and animated to induſtry, and new adventurers allured from land, each ſhip might be allowed a ſmall band of their national muſic.

To this plan there may be many objections; but I muſt confeſs I cannot ſee any material one: if the principle is admitted, the arrangement will eaſily follow, which I leave to the wiſdom of thoſe noblemen and gentlemen who have ſo laudably and liberally ſubſcribed large ſums for the purpoſe of promoting the fiſheries in Scotland. The great object to be attended to, is, the proper application of the fund. Emulation is the firſt ſpring of activity, and without ſociety there can be no competition. If the riſing generation on the weſtern coaſts of Scotland, are collected together, according to the propoſed plan, it is probable that every benefit which can be expected, will reſult from it. Emulation, in the firſt inſtance, will give vigour to the undertaking; and a few years will convince the inhabitants of that country, that they

have

have but juſt diſcovered the advantages which nature has beſtowed upon them. But, when they have taſted the benefits ariſing from their induſtry, intereſt will induce them to purſue it. I mean not, by theſe obſervations, to damp the martial ardour of the northern inhabitants of this iſland : they have ever been foremoſt in the field ; but as the exiſtence of this iſland depends upon its maritime power, I wiſh to turn their attention to this object, and there can be no doubt but the ſame intrepid ſpirit will incite them to defend their native country on the ſeas.

The Duke of Argyle's caſtle ſtands very pleaſantly, conſidering the mountainous country in which it is ſituated. It forms a ſquare with four circular turrets. One ſtory is ſunk below the ſurface of the ground: and, round this, there is a large area ſurrounded by iron rails. The caſtle has a very monaſtic appearance: though lately built, the windows of it are all turned with a Gothic arch; and it has a ſuperſtructure intended to give light to the central part of the houſe, which

which has rather a heavy appearance on the outfide, and is by no means pleafing within. There are many good rooms in the houfe, but none very large. Some of them are elegantly furnifhed, and the ceilings beautifully painted and gilded. Several of them are not yet finifhed. Though there are no hiftorical pictures, we meet with fome excellent portraits here, among which we contemplate the images of thofe patriots and heroes, the fplendour of whofe actions has raifed the family of Argyle, even in an enlightened and warlike nation, to diftinguifhed celebrity and eminence. The woods around are very extenfive, and thofe near the houfe planted with a good deal of tafte. The trees, many of which bear marks of high antiquity, are chiefly beech: there are alfo fome oaks, chefnuts, afh, with a few others. About 300 acres of land, clear of wood, is laid down chiefly for hay and grazing land: very little of it is applied to the purpofe of raifing corn; which, if we may judge from the Duke's having a large ftructure in his park for the purpofe of drying grain (the quantity of rain that falls

being

Painted by T. Garret. Heath sculp.

View of the TOWN & CASTLE of Inveraray, taken from the foot of the Hill call'd Dunacquaich.

Publish'd as th.. Act directs June 2, 1788, by G. Robinson & Partners.

being so great as to render this necessary) would be a very arduous attempt. Though the land around Inverary rises every way into mountains, it has the advantage of flat ground to the extent of about 1200 acres.

Two rivers discharge themselves into Loch-Fine, the one near the Duke's house, the other about a mile distant, over each of which there is an handsome bridge. On the top of an hill called Dunacquaich, which is 870 feet high, there stands a square building by way of a summer-house, with two windows in it. From this lofty eminence you have a very extensive view of Loch-Fine and all the neighbouring mountains, and a bird's eye prospect of the castle and all the plantations. The hill is chiefly planted with fir and birch. The trees, at the bottom of the hill, are very large; they gradually become less as you ascend; and near the top they are reduced to brush-wood. There is a tolerable road to the top of this hill, for horses, and, in different directions from the castle, you may ride through beautiful plantations

tations for several miles. About half a mile from the house is the garden, which comprehends near seven acres of ground. It has a very large hot-house and some hot walls. Cherries, and other common fruits, seem to thrive very well. Near this garden is a large building, erected with some taste, for cattle in winter, cart-houses, &c. and a number of dwelling-houses for the servants employed in husbandry. About the distance of a mile from this is another building, on an eminence, which has a very neat appearance, called the Duke's Dairy.

The town or village of Inverary is about half a mile from the castle, situated on a point of land that runs into the loch. It consists of about 200 houses, many of which, though small, are neatly built. The people are chiefly employed in fishing, which sometimes employs near 1,000 people. Although the herring be indeed a whimsical, as well as migrating animal, I must here contradict the report of the herrings having

having, in a great measure, forsaken Loch-Fine, and gone to other parts of the Scottish coast. About three miles from Inverary, there is a woollen manufactory for cloth and carpets. The person who established it failed; but the business is now conducted by another man, who has met with some success. Coals are nearly as dear here as in London, on account of the additional duty, which is a most impolitic imposition, and operates greatly against all manufactures. The price of labour at Inverary is from ten-pence to one shilling a day. On the whole, the general appearance of the castle, town, and environs of Inverary, is such as beseems the head of a great clan in a strong and mountainous country, who, without losing sight of the origin of his family in rude and warlike times, adopts the improvements of the present period.

Wednesday, July 6th. Leave Inverary. After getting out of the Duke of Argyle's woods, which extend three miles from his house up the river, the road is quite open and dreary, passing over a number of inferior hills, surrounded by
moun-

mountains, and unenlivened by the fight of a single tree or fhrub. In the intervening bottoms or flats, fome attempts are here and there vifible at cultivation, of which they appear to be abundantly capable. About eight miles from Inverary fall in at Clandifh with Loch-Awe, of which we have a beautiful view. On this part of the Loch there are eight iflands, fome covered with verdure, fome with wood, and others, which are rocky, with large fir-trees. Here alfo the loch is finely indented by promontories, advancing and fpreading into it a great way, and joined to the main land only by a narrow ifthmus. Thefe, with the iflands, form a profpect highly variegated and pleafant. On the eaft fide of the loch there is a great deal of land fit for corn, and fome of it is applied to that purpofe: but what feems beft adapted to the genius of the people, is grazing. A great number of black cattle are reared here, and a ftill greater number of fheep. On the fide of the loch ftands a well-built modern houfe, called Hay-field. This houfe formerly belonged to a Mr. Campbell, who had a caftle

upon

upon one of the iflands, the ruins of which are ftill perceptible. At the north end of the loch there is a large caftle, belonging to the Earl of Breadalbane, now falling to ruin. This, in barbarous times, was the antient den or ftronghold of the family, from which they iffued forth, at the head of their retainers, like the princes and heroes of Homer, and like thofe of all uncivilized times and countries, to commit occafional depredations on their neighbours. The prefent poffeffor has the happinefs to live in a milder age, and one more fuited to the natural benignity of his difpofition. The fculking place of his remote anceftors is abandoned. The Earl of Breadalbane, following the example of his noble predeceffor, while he opens his eyes and his fortune to the general good of every part of the country, exercifes an elegant hofpitality in his charming refidence at Loch-Tay, which fhews how much the beauty and magnificence of nature may ftill be improved by art and cultivated tafte.

In the vicinity of Loch-Awe, the moft antient patrimony of the family of Breadalbane,

albane, they now poſſeſs a country near thirty miles in extent. The preſent Lord Breadalbane has let out his land, at the upper part of the lake, on long leaſes, on which the tenants are building comfortable houſes. This muſt be productive of much good to the landlord, his tenants, and the country at large: for, by making it the intereſt of thoſe people to cultivate and improve the land, they will be induſtrious, the landlord will be more certain of his rent, and the country at large will be benefited by an increaſe of population. There are a great many inhabitants about this loch now; but their numbers, by well directed induſtry, might eaſily be trebled.

Dalmally, pleaſantly ſituated on a large river, that has its ſource in the Black Mount, near the upper end of Loch-Awe, into which it falls, is a large ſtraggling village. The miniſter has a tolerable houſe, and an income of 100l. beſides a glebe of about forty acres, of pretty good land. The inn here, which is kept by one Hiſlop, is a very good one.

Labour

Labour in this country is from ten-pence to one shilling a day. In a neighbouring mountain, called Chruachan, there is a lead mine, which they have just begun to work, and met with very good success.

Thursday, July 7th. Leave Dalmally, and go to Oban. From Dalmally to Bun-Awe the road winds round the top of Loch-Awe, on the side of a mountain, covered for the most part with trees. From the road, the descent to the water, which is a thousand feet, is, in most places, nearly perpendicular. Yet, there is not any parapet wall on the side towards the loch, to prevent your falling over, which makes it exceedingly dangerous for carriages, or even for horses, if they are not very quiet. This road extends near eight miles, when a river runs out of the loch, of most astonishing rapidity, roaring through rocks and loose stones, till it loses itself in an arm of the sea, known by the name of Loch-Etive, at the upper end of which Bun-Awe is situated. Here the Furnels Company have

an

an houfe and place for making charcoal: for which purpofe they have purchafed a great quantity of the neighbouring woods. Above this place, is the high mountain before-mentioned, called Chruachan. From Taynuld and Bun-Awe, the road bends a little inward into the country, from Loch-Etive, paffing over a number of fmall hills, which have been covered with oak and birch, though the wood is now moftly cut down for the purpofe of making charcoal. Among thefe hills, as in a great many other places in Scotland, you frequently difcover the ftumps of large trees, which prove, that very large timber has grown here formerly, and are fo many incentives to the gentlemen of Scotland to make plantations of foreft trees, fince what has flourifhed in one period, may alfo flourifh in another. The land here-about belongs chiefly to Campbell of Lochniel, but it is let on leafe to the Furnefs Company.

About two miles from Oban, there is an old ruinous caftle, with a fmall modern houfe built on the top of it.

In

In this old castle, which is called Dunstaffnage, there lives a gentleman of the name of Campbell. A little further, on the point of a rock, are the ruins of Dunolly-Castle, said to have been the residence of the first kings of Scotland. About a mile from this, at the bottom of a small bay, lies the village of Oban, which contains two or three tolerable houses. Here there are a few fishing-boats, chiefly for the fishing of herrings: a business which is carried on with some success, and which would undoubtedly be attended with more, if duly encouraged by the gentlemen of the country, to whom it would prove of great advantage. But, it would seem, that there is, in the gentlemen of this part of the country, as in the Highlands in general, a disposition to keep the lower class of people in as abject a state as possible. While this humour remains, neither commerce nor agriculture can possibly flourish. One Stevenson, who keeps a public house here, of the very worst sort, is the only man of enterprize in the place: he has built four vessels,

vessels, from 100 to 150 tons, which he employs in the coasting trade to Greenock, and other places. Having no competitor, he is making money very fast.

Friday, July 8th. We went from Dalmally to Oban, with an intention of going to the Isle of Mull, and visiting Staffa: and this I was the more desirous of doing, that I had seen such basaltic appearances as are said to distinguish that island, on a large scale, in the Straits of Sunda: a circumstance that might have suggested some comparisons, and led to some observations. But, finding, that without abundance of time, and proper introductions to the people of Mull, this would be a difficult and dangerous attempt, we relinquish our design, leave Oban, and go to Appin, which is about twelve miles distant. In the course of this ride we are obliged to cross two ferries with our horses, which is not a very pleasant undertaking, the currents being very rapid. The road is, in general, tolerably good. We have a fine view of Mull, Lismore, and several smaller islands. Lismore is the most

fertile

fertile of all the Hebrides. Though the soil be, in general, very thin, and in some places not more than an inch above the rocks, which are all slate, it produces a great quantity of corn of all kinds. Pass by the Laird of Lochniel's house, which seems to be a pretty good one, and is surrounded by large plantations. A little further onward, lives another Campbell, called the Laird of Arde, who has also a good house, and well sheltered by wood. To the north of this house is an inlet of the sea, forming a small bay, with two or three islands, on one of which are the ruins of an old castle belonging to the Laird of Arde. This den is remarkable only for being nearly as large as the island on which it stands. It serves to shew in what miserable holes the people of former times were obliged to hide themselves. Opposite to this small island is the village of Appin: and, about a mile again from this is Mr. Seaton's house, beautifully situated on an eminence, which commands a view of Lismore, with all the islands down to the Sound of Mull, and the chain of mountains which run up to Fort William. On the north-west side of Loch-Lhynn, great pains have been taken by Mr. Seaton to lay out his grounds, and raise plantations, which are very extensive. There is a great deal of grass-land about this place, and some oats and barley, which look strong and flourishing. The house is an exceedingly good one, kept neat, and commodiously furnished, as we experienced, by having very comfortable lodging and beds in it. Between Oban and Appin there is a great deal of low grazing land, and more corn than I have yet seen, in an equal space, in the Highlands.

Saturday, July 9th. Leave Appin, in the morning, and ride some distance by the water side, through Mr. Seaton's land, where great attention seems to be paid to agriculture, and particularly to keep the land clear of weeds. The manure applied, which is shell-sand and lime, seems to answer very well, as the crops are strong and healthy. In short, this country, with the roads that open and lead through it, bear evident marks of liberal

and

and patriotic proprietors; for misery and wretchedness are banished from hence, though they are still too visible, almost every where else throughout the Highlands.

Ride by the water side ten miles to Ballyhulish Ferry, where there is a small house, in which we were obliged to stay some time, being wet through when we came to it. The road in general, for such a mountainous and rocky country, is tolerably good. In the afternoon, ride through Glencoe, on each side of which are the most tremendous precipices I ever beheld in any part of the world. Torrents of water falling from these in all shapes and directions, form at the bottom a large and rapid river. As we passed through the glen, it blew a storm. Sometimes the craggy mountains were hid in black clouds, and, at others, visible through the mist, which served to aggravate the gloom of this awful place, and render it truly horrible. This seemed a fit scene for the massacre of 1691, which leaves a stain either on the memory of King William, or that of his minifters, or on both. At the foot of thefe precipitous mountains, there is much verdure, but the fides are fo perpendicular, that fcarcely even a goat can feed upon them. In the middle of the glen there are two or three miferable huts. The ftumps of great numbers of large trees remain in feveral parts of the glen. At the upper part, the fide of one mountain is ftill covered with firs: and where ever peat is dug, many large trees are found, which fhews, that this has been formerly a foreft.

Sunday, 10th July. After getting out of Glencoe, which is ten miles long, you may fee the King's Houfe, at the diftance of three miles, fituated on the fide of a rapid river. Around this lonely hut, for twenty miles in each direction, there feems to be no habitation, nor food for man or beaft. This houfe is fo ill attended to by the old rafcal who lives in it, that there is not a bed fit to fleep in, nor any thing to eat, notwithftanding that he has it rent-free, and is allowed

nine

nine pounds per annum by Government. In the morning leave this curſed place, and ride to Fort-William, twenty-four miles of very bad road, over two mountains; one at Auchnafie, called the Devil's Stair-caſe; the other at Kinloch-Leven, at the head of the lake of that name. About four miles ſouth of Fort-William is a very good grazing farm, on the Lochiel eſtate, called Loch-Andrava, of conſiderable extent, which produces the fineſt graſs I have ſeen in the Highlands.

Monday, 11th July. Viſit Fort-William, built in King William's reign. The preſent fort, which is a triangle, has two baſtions, and is capable of admitting a garriſon of 800 men, but not to be defended againſt any attack. Several hills near it command the whole fort, and the north ſide of it is quite open, the wall having lately fallen down. There are now two companies of infantry in it. About a mile from Fort-William is Inverlochy, an old caſtle, with large round towers, supposed to have been built by Edward I. In 790 Inverlochy was one of the seats of the kings of Scotland. About a mile from this castle, on the river Lochy, which empties itself into the sea at Fort-William, is a salmon fishery, the joint property of Lochiel and the Duke of Gordon: 200 barrels, containing, each, from twenty-five to twenty-seven fish, have been taken this year, which is reckoned a very successful fishing. These barrels have been sold as high as seven pounds, but produce now only five pounds, ten shillings, which will bear a profit of about forty shillings. This fishery is farmed by four men, who pay 150l. per annum for it, and for this sum have land into the bargain, which produces 50l. per annum to them. Therefore, I suppose, the fishery must be very profitable, though they do not take the means to fish the river properly. The quality of this salmon is equal to that of the Severn.

Tuesday, 12th July. Ride by the side of Lochiel to Mr. Cameron of Fassifern's house.
A part

A part of the estate of Lochiel, which lies on each side of this loch, has exceedingly good grazing land to the tops of the hills. The lower ground is a light sandy soil, which would produce very good corn, especially as a great quantity of sea-weed is thrown on the shore, which, mixed with lime, makes good manure. The lime, indeed, is not upon the spot, but is brought from the Island of Lismore in stones, and landed at Lochiel for three shillings per ton. At present, the weed which is thrown on the shore is converted to another use, which probably may be more beneficial to the proprietor than putting it on the land. It is cut once in three years, and burnt into kelp, for making glass. Mr. Cameron makes about sixteen tons of this triennially. It is sold, sometimes, for six pounds per ton on the spot, which must produce a good profit, as the only drawback, is the labour, which is one shilling a day. The estate of Lochiel to the north-west reaches all the way to Loch-Arkek, where

there

there is an extent of wood near twelve miles long, all firs: and, at the upper end of Lochiel is a very good oak wood, of near 200 acres. The eafy communication with the water and the fea, muft make the timber of confiderable value, if fuffered to grow to a large fize; but the growth of trees has been much neglected. The whole country being turned into pafture land, for the more immediate profit arifing from grazing, has prevented the wood from getting up, which it would do naturally, if it were only protected from the cattle, as clearly appears from feveral fpots about Faffifern's houfe, where the cattle are not fuffered to go, being covered with very fine oak and birch. Were this fimple plan adopted, either by inclofures or otherwife, in the worft part of the eftate, where grazing is not fo profitable, in the courfe of ten years woods might be raifed which would be very profitable. As climate here is fo much complained of, and the ripening of the corn is a matter of great uncertainty, the grazing ground

ground might, at a small expence at first, be made more productive than it is at present, by adopting the method used in Derbyshire, of large enclosures, where grass will always grow better than when it is entirely open. This would feed more black cattle, and employ more people to attend them, than sheep do, the rearing of which, I clearly see, if continued to its present extent, will depopulate the whole country; for one family can attend as many sheep as several miles will graze.

> Ill fares the land, to hast'ning ills a prey,
> While wealth accumulates, and men decay;
> Princes and lords may flourish or may fade;
> A breath can make them, as a breath has made:
> But a bold peasantry, their country's pride,
> When once destroy'd, can never be supply'd.

Another plan is absolutely necessary for the improvement of all this country, which is, to grant long leases to the tenants, and to make it their interest to live at home and cultivate the land. By these means, the estates would,

would, in time, be greatly benefited, the landlord might raife his rents without oppreffing the tenant, and thofe people who are now, to all appearance, truly miferable and wretched, rendered comfortable and happy. The oppofite plan to this is ftill the prevailing cuftom in moft parts of the Highlands. The chieftain lets the land in large lots, to the inferior branches of the family, all of whom muft fupport the dignity of lairds. Thefe renters let the land out in fmall parcels, from year to year, to the lower clafs of people, and, to fupport their dignity, fqueeze every thing out of them they can poffibly get, leaving them only a bare fubfiftence. Until this evil is obviated, Scotland can never improve.

That part of the Lochiel eftate which goes down from Fort-William to the ferry at Bally-hulifh, contains a quantity of very good grazing land, and will produce any thing that may be wifhed for, fuch as carrots, turnips, or cabbages, for feeding cattle in winter,

ter, &c. Great quantities of very fine potatoes are now growing upon it, as flourishing as any in England. By the culture of such plants and roots, more black cattle may be fed: for the great drawback in this business at present, is the want of provender in winter. Near Loch-Leven is a very good slate quarry, which in some measure supplies the neighbouring country, and some of it is sent coastways to different parts. Mr. Seaton has two on the opposite shore, which rather diminish its value: however, it may be turned to a very good account, by adopting a new and more comfortable stile of habitations in the Highlands, for the poor people, who cannot now be said to live in houses. No Kamskatka hut can be worse than a Highlander's. Those dreadful abodes must often be the cause of disease and death.

The farm of Bennevis is a very good one for grazing, and other purposes. On the banks of the River Lochy is a great extent of flat land, several hundred acres. This is

at

at present covered with a sort of moss, but has a sandy soil under it, which, by means of sea-weed or lime, may be converted into good land in the course of two or three years. Those manures destroy the moss in one year: the next, tolerable potatoes may be raised; and the third, oats or barley. It may then be laid down in grass. At the upper end of Lochiel is a salmon fishery: but nets only are used, and few fish are taken.

Wednesday, 13th July. The town of Maryborough has a good many tolerable houses in it, and contains about 500 people, who have actually no employment, but a little herring-fishing in the season. The only mode, in my opinion, which can be adopted to make them industrious, is, to establish amongst them a woollen manufactory. This country produces a great quantity of wool, which is now sent to Glasgow and Liverpool to be wrought into cloth, &c. A manufactory of wool would render the articles

ticles of dress much cheaper, and give activity to a set of men, lost to the world and to themselves in the most torpid and miserable indolence. The communication from hence to the sea is too obvious to admit of any illustration. Ships of any size may come up to Fort-William: but the passages among the islands are dangerous, from rapid tides and currents, and those storms and hard squalls to which all mountainous countries are subject. Yet it certainly may be navigated, and, in the summer months, with ease. At Fort-William there is great abundance of peat for fuel, particularly on the Lochiel estate, not three miles from the town, whither it is brought in boats. Coals also may be landed here tolerably cheap. Fish of various sorts are caught here in great plenty: salmon, turbot, herrings, haddocks, whitings, &c. &c.

To the westward of Lochiel is a considerable estate, called Clanronnald, belonging to Macdonald, who also possesses the greater part of the ifland of South Uift, which, by the article of kelp alone, produces 1500l. a year.

Thurfday, 14th July. Leave Fort-William, and go to Letter-Findlay, fourteen miles of very bad road, and rather hilly. Pafs over High-Bridge, built by General Wade over the River Spean: two of the arches are ninety-five feet high. This is a very rapid river, running between high and perpendicular rocks into Loch-Lochy, which is fourteen miles long, and two broad. This loch empties itfelf into the weftern fea, at Fort-William, as Loch-Oich does through Loch-Nefs, into the eaftern, at Invernefs. From Fort-William to the weft part of Loch-Lochy, there is a great quantity of good grazing land, the gras being of a moderate height. The mountains on the north of the loch are of vaft height, and barren, except near the bottom, where there is fome good grafs. On the fouth fide of the loch there are good fheep-walks, and the land is, in various places, covered with wood. When you firft

come

come upon Loch-Lochy, you have a view into Loch-Arkek; and upon the oppofite fhore, near the entrance into Loch-Arkek, ftood Achnacarrie, the feat of Lochiel, burnt in 1746. The road from this place ftretches eight miles, on the fide of Loch-Lochy, and is fometimes carried through very beautiful woods of aller and birch. After paffing Loch-Lochy, a very fhort diftance brings you to Loch-Oich, a narrow lake, prettily indented, and adorned with fmall, wooded iflands. On the north fhore, near the middle of the lake, is Glen-Garie, the feat of Mr. Macdonald, a modern, though odd-built houfe. Near this ftand the ruins of an old caftle, fituated on a rock. This place is prettily wooded, and the land up the glen feems to be well cultivated.

After leaving this loch, you travel about four miles to Fort-Auguftus, which is fituated on a plain at the head of Loch-Nefs, between the Rivers Tarff and Oich. Over the laft of thefe, there is a bridge of three arches,

arches, well built, which opens a communication with the north. Fort-Auguſtus is a ſmall fortreſs, formed by four baſtions, and is capable of containing about 400 men. It is not capable of any defence, being commanded by ſeveral places at no great diſtance. Near the fort is a ſmall village, and a tolerable inn; and below it, a little pier, which affords ſhelter for ſmall veſſels and boats, that come from Inverneſs to ſupply the garriſon. The mountains on each ſide of Fort-Auguſtus are very rocky and barren: nor is there much grazing or corn-land in the bottoms.

Friday, July 15. Leave Fort-Auguſtus, and aſcend a very long hill to the ſouth of the fort, which is near three miles to the top; on reaching the ſummit of which, you are preſented with a view of numberleſs hills and mountains of almoſt barren rock. In the vallies, or rather pits, may be ſeen a few acres of grazing land, and a ſmall quantity of corn. On the top of this mountain

is

is Loch-Tarff, about a mile wide, with several small islands in it, on some of which you see a few shrubs. This loch sends forth the River Tarff, which runs down to Fort-Augustus, swelled in its passage by several small streams. Ride nine miles over this barren country, and arrive at the celebrated fall of Foyers, at the upper part of the glen, which is beautifully covered with birch-trees. Above the fall is a bridge built over the river upon two perpendicular rocks, the top of the arch near 100 feet from the level of the water; and just above the bridge, the whole body of the Tarff falls near fifty feet perpendicular into the glen. Near a quarter of a mile below this bridge is the large fall, which is near two hundred feet, and the water afterwards runs into Loch-Ness, over large and rugged rocks. On a promontory close by this river, a gentleman of the name of Fraser, has a house pleasantly situated, which commands a good view of the loch, and the mountains on each side. About a mile

mile from the Fall of Foyers, the road is carried through a very beautiful birch wood, to the General's Hut, a very indifferent public houfe, where we were obliged to dine on very bad fare. Near this are the remains of an old kirk, where many of the Frafers lie expofed to the rude infults of man and beaft. After leaving the General's Hut, the road goes for twelve miles by the fide of Loch-Nefs, through a beautiful fhrubbery of birch, oak, and allers. The oppofite fide of the loch is formed by very high mountains, moftly covered with heath. At the lower part of the loch, which is twenty-four miles long, and at fome places a mile wide, are many plantations of fir, fome of them very extenfive, but none of the trees above fifteen or twenty years old. Some hollies, and a great deal of juniper and furze, grow at the lower part of the loch. This furze is the firft I have feen in the Highlands. The plantations of fir are continued all the way to Invernefs, which is about five miles from

the

the lower end of Loch-Nefs, where it forms a river which falls into the Murray-Firth.

On the north fide of this great expanfe of water, where it is indented by a promontory of folid rock, ftands Caftle-Urquhart, once the feat of the Cummins, at one period the moft powerful clan in Scotland. The lake, with its woody borders, the lofty mountains within which it is embofomed, and the eafy tranfition of ideas, by means of the lake, to the forts, and to the town of Invernefs, render this fpot one of the moft charming that the imagination can conceive. The foil between the lower part of Loch-Nefs and Invernefs is very fandy, but produces tolerable corn. In the River-Nefs much falmon is caught. The fifhery is let to the London fifhmongers.

Invernefs is a town of confiderable magnitude, faid to contain about 11,000 inhabitants. Some of the houfes in it are tolerably built, but the ftreets narrow and dirty. It is fituated on a plain between the Murray Firth and the River Nefs. Ships of 4 or 500 tons

tons can ride within a mile of the town, and, at high tide, vessels of 200 tons can come up to the quay, which, though small, is made safe and convenient. The principal business carried on here is the spinning of thread, making linen and woollen cloth for their own consumption, and sacking for exportation. Several large buildings have been erected for those purposes, and much business is carried on in private houses. On the north, near the town, are the remains of Oliver's Fort, which was made of mud. Three of the bastions are still remaining. This fort was well situated, for it commands the whole town, and might at any time be surrounded by water. Several of the factory houses are now built within it, and a part of it forms the bason for the reception of vessels. On the south side of the town, on an eminence, stood old Fort-George, taken and blown up by the Highlanders in 1746. Just below this place is a handsome bridge of seven arches over the River Ness. Several places round

round Inverness command beautiful views, particularly a hill covered with firs called Tomnaheurich. From this hill you may see the whole town, the Murray-Firth, the River Ness, and a variety of neighbouring mountains. There is a great deal of corn raised about Inverness, particularly oats and beans. The soil is light and sandy, and there are great complaints here of the want of rain: so very different from, and yet so near is the climate to that about Fort-William. The want of rain, in this part of Scotland, may be accounted for as follows: the mountains on the south-west, from which the rain generally comes, are so exceedingly high, that the clouds are arrested, and shed among them the greatest part of their moisture. Those western mountains are also so strangely formed, and heaped up to the sky in so many perpendicular points, that they naturally occasion eddies round them, and draw the wind in various directions, making as it were a kind of vortex: so that the clouds cannot possibly escape them. By this means the eastern part of Scotland, which lies in their direction, is prevented from receiving the quantity of rain by which it would be watered. This part of the country, at present, bears evident marks of drought, from the top of Loch-Nefs all the way to the eastward, while every part of the West Highlands is refreshed with rain even in superabundance.

The island of Great Britain, between Invernefs and Fort-William, assumes a form that is very extraordinary and curious. It is deeply indented on either side, and nearly divided by water, which is mostly, and might easily be made navigable all the way. But a considerable commerce alone could make a return suitable to the expence of doing so. Loch-Nefs, Loch-Oich, and Loch-Lochy, which are all navigable, might easily be united with each other, by canals, and form a communication between the two seas. The land which separates these lochs is low, and a canal might easily be made from one to the

the other. These lochs, from Inverness to Fort-William, are bounded by high mountains on each side, and from both the western and the eastern point of view, exhibit the appearance of the island being intersected by water.

Saturday, 16th, July. Leave Inverness, and ride fifteen miles, part of it over Culloden Moor: pass by Culloden-House, the seat of Mr. Forbes, and the ruins of Cauder-Castle; and have a very good view of Fort-George, a strong and regular fortress. The barracks here are handsome, forming several good streets. This fort is situated on a low and narrow neck of land, running into the Murray-Firth, and compleatly commands the entrance into the harbour. The land between Inverness and Nairn is quite low and sandy.

Nairn is a small town, situated on an eminence near the sea. The houses are built of stone, and some of them pretty good. The north-east end of the town is composed of mise-

miserable Highland huts. Many boats belong to the people of this town, the principal employment of the men being fishing. The boats are large, and, from their construction, capable of bearing a great deal of sail. They are made rather sharp before, and continue their breadth nearly to the stern. This is a good country for corn; but the soil being sandy, the want of rain has kept the crops very backward.

Sunday, 17th July. Leave Nairn, and ride most part of the way, on the beach, by the sea-side, to Forres, a small well-built town, pleasantly situated near some little hills, and, as it lies on an eminence, capable of being kept very clean. The country about it has a chearful appearance, having a few gentlemen's seats, with some plantations about them. On a hill west of the town are the remains of a castle, and a melancholy view of a number of sand-hills, that now cover that tract of land which was formerly the estate of a Mr. Cowben, in the

parish

parish of Dyke. This inundation was occasioned by the influx of the sea, and the violence of the wind. It had been the custom to pull up the bent, a long spiry grass, near the shore, for litter for horses, by which means the sand was loosened, and gave way to the violence of the sea and wind, which carried it over several thousand acres of land. The people having been prevented from pulling up any more of the grass, the progress of the sand is now nearly stopped, and the sea has retired: but the wind has blown some of the sand from the hills over Colonel Grant's land, and destroyed near one hundred acres. A sand-bank, which is all dry at low water, runs out from this place for several miles, into the Murray-Firth. Some of the land, which has been long forsaken by the water, is now beginning to be useful again, and is turned into grazing land. At Forres, coarse linen and sewing-thread are made. About a mile from the town, on the left-hand side of the road, is a stone near

twenty

twenty feet high, called King Sweno's Stone, erected by the Scots in memory of the final retreat of the Danes. On a moor, about four miles further, Shakespear places the rencounter of Macbeth and the Wierd Sisters; and it is judiciously chosen, for all the women in this part of the country have the appearance of midnight hags. They only want the cauldron and the broom-stick to compleat them for the stage. In our way from Forres to Elgin, pass by the ruins of Kinloss-Abbey, founded by David I. in 1150. Near this place Duffus, King of Scotland, was said to be murdered by thieves. All the country between Forres and Elgin is very barren; mostly black heath and sand mixed with gravel. In some places there is a tolerable crop of beare, which is a poor sort of barley, and oats: but the ground much in want of rain. Near Elgin is a large moor, or moss, which the possessor is draining; by which he employs a great number of people, and in time may probably reap some benefit to himself.

For

For where a mofs grows over fand, it may, in a few years, be brought into good grazing land. About half a mile from Elgin is a very large plantation of firs, called Quarry-Wood.

Elgin, a town about the fize of Forres, has a few good houfes in it. Of the cathedral, a very beautiful old ruin, part of two towers, the weft entrance, and the chancel, ftill remain, though much mutilated: however, there is enough to fhew the exquifite workmanfhip with which it was formed, and whoever fees it, muft lament the rude violence of the Reformers, that brought it to defolation. On the weft of the town, on a hill, ftood an old caftle, which, from its fituation, would command the town. Of this ftructure, a few heaps of ftones are now only remaining. The people here, as in all the little towns on this coaft from Invernefs, are employed in making thread and linen cloth, chiefly for their own confumption. All thefe towns, Invernefs, Nairn, Forres, and Elgin, have a very difmal appearance, being all built of

dark

dark stone: nor can they claim the merit of being very clean, and Elgin, in filthiness, exceeds them all.

Monday, 18th July. Leave Elgin, and go to Fochabers, through several miles of very good corn land; the soil sandy; the crops now on the ground chiefly beare and oats, with some few acres of wheat. About five miles from Elgin, on the left, is a gentleman's seat, with very extensive plantations of firs, upon land which, in a few years, might be made very fit for any kind of grain. By alloting certain portions, rent free, for eight or nine years, to poor families, they would be able to maintain themselves, improve the land, and promote population. It is impossible to avoid observing the injudicious manner in which the Scots have made plantations: nor can I possibly account for it in any other way than by considering it as the effect of passion. They have been continually ridiculed by the English, for having no trees in their country. Some men,

there-

therefore, determined to be laughed at no longer, have gone home, and inſtead of planting a variety of trees, and placing them ſo as to be a ſcreen to the land, and an ornament to the country, they have turned great portions of their eſtates into foreſts of Scotch firs, which are but ugly trees at beſt, and which grow ſo nearly of a height, and are placed ſo cloſe together, that the country ſtill looks, at a diſtance, as if there was not a tree in it. The particular plantation I have juſt mentioned, is at a ſufficient diſtance from the houſe, to admit of converſion into corn-land without interfering with the pleaſure-ground: therefore, I would recommend it to the owner to cut all the trees down, and make the uſe of it I have mentioned. It is a melancholy reflection, that people are leaving the Highlands daily, and tranſporting themſelves to America, while thouſands of acres are lying waſte, which might be made productive to the owner, and maintain numberleſs families.

Croſs

Cross the River Spey at Fochabers, where there is a ferry-boat, but no bridge. This, I believe, is the most rapid river in Scotland. After heavy rains it carries every thing before it. At Fochabers is Gordon-Castle, a very large and elegant building. The centre of the house is old. The north-east front is regular. The south-west front has a square tower in the middle, which is considerably higher than the top of the house; the wings, which are new, are very elegant. The whole front extends near 350 feet, and has upwards of 120 windows. The situation of the house is low, and rather damp. The park, though not extensive, has many fine old trees in it, but planted without taste or judgment. All the grounds about it are in a very unfinished state. The hills above the house are all planted with fir. As to the inside of the house, I can say nothing. The Duchess being at home, we did not chuse to intrude upon her. The old town of Fochabers consists of miserable huts, but a new one is begun, in which

which are several good houses, and two tolerable inns. At this place there is an establishment for making sewing-thread, in which about fifty girls are employed. From Fochabers to Cullen is twelve miles, a very fine corn country all the way, and the crops of wheat, beare, and oats, very flourishing and strong. The soil, in this part of the country, has in it a mixture of clay. Some fields of grey pease are sown here, and seem to thrive very well. On this road are a number of small houses, belonging to the Gordons, being in the neighbourhood of the Duke.

Cullen is a small poor town, without one good house in it, pleasantly situated on the side of a small hill, under which is Cullenhouse, a seat of the Earl of Findlater, standing on the edge of a glen. The plantations round it are very extensive. The house is very antient and large, but there are no good rooms in it, nor any pictures, except a few tolerable portraits. A bridge of one arch

arch, of seventy feet high, is thrown over the glen juſt by the houſe, at the bottom of which runs a rapid ſtream. In the evening paſs by Portſoy, a neat little fiſhery town, on a ſmall promontory, running into the ſea. Arrive at Bamff at night. The country between Cullen and Bamff is well cultivated, and incloſed, in ſome places, by ſtone dykes. It produces a great quantity of beare and oats, and a ſmall proportion of wheat and grey peaſe. The ſoil is remarkably good, and the effects of good huſbandry are very viſible. Moſt of the cottages, and particularly the farm-houſes, are built of ſtone, and covered with tiles or ſlate: a comfortable ſight, to which we have not been accuſtomed ſince we entered Scotland. The poor people in all the weſtern part of it, are ſtill living in miſerable huts, a few of which are to be ſeen here.

Bamff is pleaſantly ſituated on the ſide of a hill, cloſe to the ſea. There are ſeveral ſtreets in it, and one which is very decent.

The

The harbour is but indifferent. The salmon-fishing here, in the River Divenon, amounts to 1000l. per annum. Near the town is Duff-house, the seat of the Earl of Fife, a very large pile of building, with a square tower at each end. The front is richly ornamented with carving. The rooms are all small, and the best apartments are not yet finished. The plantation and walks about this house are laid out with more taste and elegance, than any I have seen in Scotland. A beautiful river, called the Dive, runs through the grounds, and near the house is an elegant bridge over it, of nine arches, built by Government. All the neighbouring hills are covered with pine. Opposite to Bamff is a little town, called Macduff, belonging to the Earl of Fife, who is taking much pains to improve it, and is building a pier for the coasting vessels, which, when finished, will be safe and commodious.

Tuesday, 19th July. Leave Bamff, and go through two small villages, called New Deer and Old Deer, to Peterhead. From Bamff to New Deer, about sixteen miles. The land here belongs chiefly to Lord Fife; a great part of it is in a high state of improvement. It is mostly corn land, though there is some fit for the fattening of cattle, to which use a part of it is applied. Many of the bullocks are so large, as to amount, when fattened, to the value of 25l. At Old Deer is the remains of an old abbey, and near it is held a large fair annually for cattle, for which they were preparing as we passed. From this place to Peterhead, a space of sixteen miles, the soil is a cold stiff clay: the crops very thin, and backward.

Wednesday, July 20. Peterhead is a neat little town, situated on a peninsula. It contains about 3000 people. They have lately built a new pier, of granite, which cost 8000l. The harbour will now contain about twenty vessels. They have twelve feet water at the pier-head. The commerce here is very considerable to the Baltic and Dantzic, for deals, hemp,

hemp, &c. Seventeen veſſels are employed in this and the coaſting trade, and three large ſloops are annually ſent to fiſh among the Weſtern Iſlands, and the Hebrides, where they catch great quantities of cod and ling, which they ſalt, and ſell to the inhabitants of the Weſtern Highlands. There is a great deal of fiſh caught alſo at Peterhead, and Peterburgh : near 2000 barrels of cod annually, which is ſent to different towns on the coaſt, and ſome of it to London. At Peterhead is a very good mineral ſpring, which is conſidered as very efficacious in removing any complaint in the bowels. It operates as a very ſtrong diuretic. Near the ſpring is a very good ball-room, under which there are two ſalt-water baths. In the ſeaſon this is a place of polite reſort. The town is neat, and well built, and the inn a very good one. Eight hundred people are employed here, in a factory for ſewing-thread. The girls earn from five-pence to fifteen-pence per diem. The harbour is ſafe,

and

and eafy of accefs. Turbot are frequently fold here for four-pence, weighing twenty pounds. From Peterhead go to Bownefs, a fmall fifhing-town, where are the celebrated Bullers, or Boilers of Buchan: a great hollow in a rock projecting into the fea, open at the top, through which you may fee the boats laying in a bafon, below which is a good harbour for them in bad weather. About two miles fouth of this place, is Slane's Caftle, the feat of the Earl of Errol, a very old houfe, forming a quadrangle in the middle. Its fituation is very curious, being upon the top of a rock, almoft perpendicular from the fea, and entirely expofed to the violence of the winds from the eaftward. In a ftorm, the fpray of the fea actually dafhes upon the houfe: but when it was built, this inconvenience was trifling, when the fecurity it afforded from favage neighbours was confidered. It is, two thirds, furrounded by water. On the acceffible fide, there was a ditch and drawbridge, but now both are deftroyed.

ſtroyed. The houſe has little or no furniture in it, and is much neglected. The gardens are turned into corn-fields. Near the houſe are ſome remarkable rocks, on which thouſands of ſea-birds build their neſts. One of thoſe rocks forms a natural arch of at leaſt ſixty feet high. About half a mile north of the houſe is a mineral well, which ſeems to have the ſame quality as that at Peterhead. From Slanes go to Ellan, a ſmall village, where the Earl of Aberdeen has a houſe, with ſome tolerable plantations about it: but we were refuſed leave to walk through any of them, or to ſee the inſide of the houſe: the only inſtance of this ſort we have met with in Scotland. From Ellan to Aberdeen is ſixteen miles, of very bad country. The greateſt part is black heath, full of rocks and large ſtones; ſo that the plough, except in a few ſpots, cannot enter it. At the north end of Old Aberdeen, is an elegant Gothic arch, turned over the River Don; a large

deep

and deep river running through a glen, till it comes near the fea.

Old Aberdeen confifts of one ftreet only, and the houfes are very indifferent. There is a College, called King's College, founded by James IV. At prefent about 150 ftudents belong to it, eighty of whom have apartments in the college. The reft muft lodge out of it, for want of room. Commons are provided for them in the college, but they are at liberty to eat in or out of it as they think proper. This building is by no means uniform or ftriking, except the top of the tower, which is turned in two arches, fupporting the crowns, and has rather an elegant appearance. The library is a good room, and contains an excellent collection of antient and modern books, with fome very curious old manufcripts. The chapel, which joins the library, is very old, and much out of repair. The hall is a large well-proportioned room, very ill furnifhed; but it has fome good portraits in it. There are profefsors here of all the sciences, and their salaries are but small. Hence, they pay great attention, I am told, to their different departments. If a man has a disposition to obtain learning and information, he may acquire them here at a small expence; and without this disposition, he will acquire them no where. Their vacation happened at this time, which lasts six months. During the other six, lectures are continually read, and the students are called on, as at schools, to give an account of their lessons.

New Aberdeen, situated between the Rivers Don and Dee, is a large and well-built city, adjoining to the old town of that name. Some of the streets are wide, and the houses lofty and spacious: they are all built of granite, the same kind of stone which is sent from hence to pave the streets of London. This stone is so hard, that no people can work it except those who have been accustomed to it from their youth. The instrument they use
is

is very simple : it is a kind of hammer with two sharp points. The principal art in working this stone seems to me to be perseverance. And who will deny that an Aberdeen's man possesses this quality ? The stone, however, when it is worked, looks well, and must be very durable. The public buildings here, are two large kirks, close together, and Gordon's School, at some distance from the city, with a large garden round it. This school, which is a handsome stone building, supports and educates eighty boys, in reading, writing, arithmetic, French, &c. A college here, founded by Earl Marischal, about the same size as King's College, is attended by the same number of students, but none of those live in the college. The library here is much inferior to that of the other seminary. The hall is a handsome room, with a full length picture of Lord Bute, a half length of Lord Buchan, and some other good portraits. The museum is a small room, containing a very indifferent collection of curiosities, but

a numa number of excellent instruments for experimental philosophy. The town-hall is a spacious and elegant room. Here is also a grammar school, and an hospital, a very plain building, which sends out between 7 and 800 patients annually. The two cities of Aberdeen contain about 13,000 souls, and about 3,000 in the suburbs.

The trade of Aberdeen is chiefly to Holland and the Baltic, and a vessel or two to Oporto. Its manufactures and trade, woollen, thread, and cotton stockings, but chiefly woollen, of which they send a great quantity annually to Holland and Germany: salmon, grain, dried skate, ling, cod, &c. The pier of Aberdeen is 1200 feet long, built in a circular form, for the purpose of keeping the River Dee within certain bounds, to clear the harbour, and obtain a sufficient draught of water; which has had the desired effect, for they have now thirteen feet water over the bar, which will admit of ships of four hundred tons burthen. This pier cost 16,000l. It is very strong, and built of granite. At

Aberdeen is an exceeding good market for all forts of meat and vegetables, and a great variety of fifh. The inn kept by Mr. Smith is a very good one.

Friday, 22d July. Leave Aberdeen, and crofs the Dee, a very large river, over which is an elegant bridge of feven arches. About a mile and a half from the bridge, on the Stonehaven road, is a beautiful view of the city, with a number of neat country houfes round it. From this hill the road runs near the fea all the way to Stonehaven, and is very dreary: no trees to be feen, except now and then a fmall plantation of firs. Some few fpots are converted into corn land and grafs, but heath prevails. The huts are little better than the Highland ones.

Stonehaven is a fmall village, fituated in a rocky bay. The inhabitants are chiefly fupported by fifhing. They have four or five floops here, of forty or fifty tons burthen, which they employ in the fifhery, and go to Aberdeen, and other places on the coaft to
difpofe

difpofe of what they get. The fifh generally taken are, cod, ling, haddocks, and fkate, and fometimes they take a great quantity of dog-fifh, from which they extract oil.

About a mile from Stonehaven, to the fouth, are the ruins of Dunotter-Caftle, the antient feat of the Earls Marifchal of Scotland, on a high perpendicular rock, almoft furrounded by the fea. On the acceffible part, which is very narrow, there are three gate-ways within each other, and to each was formerly affixed a port cullife. This place, before cannon were in ufe, muft have been impregnable: it has been very large, and capable of containing feveral hundred men. Sleep at Stonehaven. The only factory here is a fmall one for canvafs, carried on by fome people of Aberdeen.

Saturday, 23d July. In the morning leave Stonehaven, and go to Inverbervie. The road runs on cliffs all the way by the fea-fide. The foil is in many places very good, and tolerably cultivated.

Inverbervie is a small village between two hills, which terminate in high cliffs towards the sea. The vale behind it is very pleasant and fertile. The people of this village are chiefly employed in making sewing-thread. Go from Inverbervie to Montrose; fifteen miles of highly cultivated land, great part of it inclosed. The wheat, beare, and oats, remarkably good; and the grass very thick. There are several good houses near the road, with tolerable plantations about them. The farm-houses, and even the cottages, in this part of the country, are well built and comfortable. Two miles from Montrose is an elegant bridge of seven arches, over the River North-Esk, built by the people of Montrose, at the expence of 6,500l. a very liberal donation to the public, for on this bridge there is no toll-gate. The King, out of the forfeited estates, granted them the aid of 800l.

Montrose is a considerable town, well built of stone, and has one very wide street in it. It is situated on a sandy plain, and close by it runs

runs the river South-Efk, which is navigable up to the town for fhips of 3 or 400 tons. Larger fhips may come in, as there are eighteen feet water over the bar, but the veffels they generally employ are about 200 tons. A great deal of coarfe linen cloth, called Ofnaburghs, is made here for exportation: alfo canvafs and fewing-thread: a great deal of malt too, is made for exportation. At Montrofe is an Englifh chapel, a neat building, with an organ in it. The town-houfe is a handfome building on porticos. To the weft of the town is a bafon, nearly two miles wide, through which runs the South-Efk River. This bafon is full at high water, and dry at half-ebbs. Were there water enough in it for veffels to lie in, it would be as convenient a harbour as any in Britain. A great quantity of falmon is caught here, in the North and South-Efk Rivers, but this year the fifhermen have been rather unfuccefsful. Montrofe is well fupplied with fifh, and provifions of all kinds. In the neighbourhood

bourhood are several country-houses, some of them belonging to the merchants of Montrose. All the country round is covered with corn.

Sunday, 24th July. Leave Montrose, and go to Forfar, twenty-three miles. Pass a small town called Brechin, where there is an old house, well surrounded by trees, belonging to Lord Panmure. Sleep at Forfar, a small town: the houses very indifferent. This seems to be the richest country in Scotland, of equal extent; for the whole of it, as far east and west as the eye can carry, and to the north as far as the Grampian Mountains, the land is covered with corn, chiefly beare and oats : the proportion of wheat appears to be small. The crops are all very thick and strong. Near the town of Forfar is a small piece of water, upon the estate of Lord Strathmore, the bottom of which is fine marl. This small spot is so valuable, that it has produced 1800l. per annum.

Monday,

Monday, 25th July. Leave Forfar in the morning, and ride fix miles to Glamis-Caftle, belonging to Lord Strathmore. This antient caftle is fituated on a plain, and furrounded by extenfive woods and plantations. The centre, and one wing of the caftle, are entire: the other wing has been taken down. The caftle is very high, with a number of curious and conical turrets on the top: there are at leaft fifty rooms in it ftill, though only part of it remains. In the centre, to which you afcend by a number of large ftone fteps, is a fpacious hall with a cove ceiling, which, with its furniture, feems to have fuffered no alteration fince the caftle was firft built, It is truly defcriptive of its former favage inhabitants. The whole of the caftle feems well calculated for the perpretation of the horrid deed which Shakefpear has recorded. In the front of the houfe are feveral large ftatues of the Stuart family, caft in lead, and a very curious fun-dial fupported by four lions.

After leaving Forfar, the road is frequently bounded by thorn hedges, a sight very unusual to us; for, except what is called the policies about the noblemen and gentlemen's houses, which are but thinly scattered, little wood, and no inclosure is to be seen. Dine at Coupar, a small village with a very bad public house. In the evening go about a mile out of the road to see the old palace of Scone, which now belongs to Lord Stormont. The gateway and part of the old front of the palace now only remain. Lord Stormont has made many additions to it by building several habitable rooms, and means occasionally to reside here. This palace, renowned for the place where the kings of Scotland were crowned, is very pleasantly situated on the bank of the River Tay, and commands a beautiful view of the river and the neighbouring hills, with part of the town of Perth.

Across the Tay, there is thrown a bridge of eleven arches, which cost about 25,000l. A large sum was contributed for this structure

ture by Government, out of the fund for making and repairing roads in North-Britain, and the revenue arising from the forfeited estates, which was seldom so well employed, being generally wasted in stipends for insolent factors, or land-stewards, or in donations to such speculative projectors, as happened to enjoy the favour of the leading men among the trustees. But, besides what was given, with equal liberality and wisdom, by Government, contributions to the amount of 17,000l. were raised in different parts of the country, all more or less concerned in an easy communication, at so centrical a situation, between the northern and southern parts of Scotland. The bridge of Perth, extended over the greatest weight of water in Britain, is a noble instance of the power of art over nature, and a glorious monument to the memory of a neighbouring nobleman, through whose exertions it was begun, continued, and happily finished. The Earl of Kinnoull, after many years spent in very honourable public life, in the course of which he took a very warm part, under the Administration of Mr. Pelham, in the abolition of hereditary jurisdictions, continued his habits of beneficent activity in retirement. His estates in the neighbourhood of Perth are beautified with commodious farm-houses for his tenants; the land divided into inclosures, and sheltered by rising hedges; and all his people, instructed by him, like the father of a numerous family, in the principles of husbandry, and indulged with leases on reasonable terms, are distinguished among their neighbours by every mark of prosperity. Loncarty, the scene of action where the founder of his family gained immortal renown, by repressing the victorious fury of the Danes, lies on the Tay, about three miles north from Perth, and is now as remarkable for the arts of peace, as it was formerly for the opposition of arms. In those fields, which are now covered with linen cloth, or luxuriant crops of wheat,

wheat, and other grain, swords, spears, and targets, occasionally dug up in the course of agriculture, and in the formation of canals for the purposes of bleaching, add every day new documents of the authenticity of the Scottish history. In the vicinity of Perth are some of the most extensive bleaching-fields to be found in Scotland: and here the linen manufacture flourishes greatly in all its branches. Here, too, the cotton manufactures begin to thrive, under the fostering care of the Duke of Athol, Mr. Graham of Balgowan, Mr. Dempster, and, above all, of that ingenious and excellent citizen, Mr. Arkwright. The river, which is navigable by ships of 200 tons, conspires with an inland situation, and that vast extent of country watered by the Ern, the Tay, the Tummel, and the Islay, of all which it is the natural port and emporium, contribute to render Perth one of the most prosperous places in North-Britain. Nor should it be forgotten, on this subject, that these favourable circumstances have been duly seconded and improved, by the industry and enterprizing spirit of certain individuals, and particularly the family of the Sandemans, and of late, by the spirited exertions of Macalpine. It may also be observed, amongst the natural prerogatives of the town of Perth, that, from its situation, it has naturally become a post for armies, in times of civil war, and a military station, in times of peace. This is the source of some of those capitals, which are at this day happily employed in manufactures and commerce. Another considerable source of prosperity to Perth, is the salmon fishery, the greatest in all Scotland, and improved to its full extent by the ingenuity and enlarged views of Mr. Richardson. The Tay, about a mile below Perth, suddenly disappears, and is lost between the lofty Cliff of Kinnoull, and the Hill of Moncrieff: so that the masts of vessels, like the neighbouring plantations of wood, seem to have sprung up from the ground, not to have been

wafted

wafted from the ocean. On the northern and the eastern banks of the Tay, from these twin hills to Dundee, lies a district of amazing fertility, called the Carse of Gowrie, twenty miles in length, and, on an average, about three miles in breadth. Two miles to the eastward of the Hill of Moncrieff, the River Ern falls into the Tay, now expanded into an estuary or frith, having a part of Fife-shire on the south, and the fertile plain just mentioned, the common granary of Perth and Dundee, on the north.

The configuration, and relative position of the Hills of Moncrieff and Kinnoull, and of the Hill of Dunsinnane, about four miles north-east from the latter, strikes the spectator, as by a sensation, with the truth of what has been remarked by natural historians, that hills lying in the same meridional direction, have their steepest and boldest faces towards the west. These distinguished eminences present, uniformly, perpendicular fronts to the south-west, and terminate, by gradual flopings, in the valleys or plains on the north and eaft. A fimilar obfervation may be made on the general fhape and fituation of all the mountains in Britain; but where three hills, fimilarly fhaped and fituated, burft upon your fight at one view, comparifons and inferences are unavoidable. The old towns in Great Britain, as well as on the Continent, are, almoft without exception, built by accident, and without a plan. Their ftreets, or lanes, are crowded and narrow, and their general *contour* is irregular. Perth and St. Andrews are among the few, if not the only antient towns in Scotland, that have been evidently formed by defign: both of them confifting of parallel and wide ftreets, joined by others croffing them at right angles. It is farther to be obferved, concerning Perth that different ftreets and lanes appear to have been very early allotted, probably from its foundation, to the different craftfmen. At this day, and as far back as memory, tradition, or written

records

records carry up the researches, and gratify the curiosity of the local antiquarian, fellow-craftsmen, with a few exceptions, are constantly found inhabiting the same quarter of the town, or the same streets. The skinners, or furriers corporation, live in one street, with certain adjacent closes and allies; the weavers in a second; the hammer-men in a third; the shop-keepers, or, as they are called, merchants, in a fourth; the butchers, before the erection of a flesh-market, in a fifth; and so on. On the north and the south sides of the town, are two extensive and beautiful fields of meadow, or pasture land, never yet subdued by the plough, bounded on the east by the river, each of them about a mile and an half in circumference, and that on the south side planted round with a double row of planes and elms, and other forest trees. A wing, or spur, according to the antient idiom of the Caledonians, of the Hill of Moncrieff, sloped down into gentle eminences, covered

with

with plantations of wood, half encircle this delightful spot on the south and the west; while the base of the Hill of Kinnoull, planted, in like manner, with trees, stretching, and uniting by slow degrees with a vast plain, bounded on the north by the Grampian Mountains, and on either hand by the ocean, shelters and adorns it on the east. That plain, which, from its large extent, is called Strathmore, is terminated on the east by the German Ocean at Stonehaven, and on the west, by the estuary of Clyde at Dunbarton. Its northern boundary has been already mentioned: its southern is formed by a range of hills, running parallel with the Grampians, but which, its contiguity being in two or three places interrupted by the course of rivers, is to be considered under three sub-divisions. The first of these, beginning our survey from the east, is, or may be, by a small extension of the term, called the Sidley Hills, rising to the southward of Forfar in Angus, and falling from

their

their height, as they ſtretch in a weſterly courſe along the northern edge of the Carſe of Gowrie, till they riſe again ſuddenly in the Hills of Kinnoull and Moncrieff, that emphatically mark the weſtern extremity of the colonade. The ſecond is the Ochills, beginning near the moſt northern and eaſterly extremity of Fife, on the ſouthern banks of the Frith of Tay, oppoſite to Dundee, and terminating in the Kippen Hills, near Stirling. The third and laſt ſub-diviſion of that range of hills which forms the ſouthern boundary of that great ſtrath, or valley, which interſects the iſland, is the Campſey Hills, which gradually ſink and diſappear near Dunbarton, and which ſhoot off a branch, in a ſouth-eaſterly direction, towards Kirkintilloch.

Between the firſt and ſecond of theſe ſubdiviſions, then, which are formed by the great rivers of the Tay and the Forth, and nearly at an equal diſtance from the eaſtern and weſtern boundaries of that ſpacious

plain

plain which runs across the island, stands the Town of Perth, celebrated in the Scottish history, as the frequent seat of Parliaments, and the residence of Kings, who exercised there the prerogative of coining money, and other acts of royalty, and from whose bounty it derived, and now enjoys, a valuable domain, as well as many immunities, rights, and privileges.

The Town of Perth, called antiently Bertha, was, in former times, situated on the northern banks of the Almon, near the junction of that river with the Tay. But, in the year 1,200, in the reign of William, the town, with the very soil on which it stood, was swept off in one night, by a dreadful inundation of the rivers. In this calamity many of the inhabitants, with their substance, lost their lives. An infant son of the King's, with his nurse, and fourteen domestics, were among the number of those that perished. A new Bertha, or, as it is now called, Perth, by a change in pronunciation

ciation incident to all living languages, was built on a fertile plain, two miles below, on the fame river. Hence the regularity and beauty of Perth, formed on a regular plan by the Court of Scotland, which held at this period, and for many years before, an intimate correspondence both with France and Italy. Nobles, princes of the blood, kings themselves left, for a time, the sequestered and rude regions of their native Caledonia, to display their valour, and acquire new accomplishments on the Continent. England, which divided Scotland from France by local situation, united it to that kingdom by the band of hostility to a common enemy. And thus, from the northerly position of Scotland, which connected it by political intrigues with the enemies of England, Scottish travellers and soldiers of fortune, imported into their country, in times of very general barbarism, some customs and modes of thinking that were either unknown, or, from animosity, rejected by their southern neighbours.

This

This conclufion, which might be fairly drawn, even by reafoning a *priori*, from moral nature, and the hiftory of nations, is placed beyond doubt, by hiftorical records, and the very texture of the Scottifh dialect; in the earlieft fpecimens of which, we meet with words of both French and Italian extraction.

There was formerly a wooden bridge at Perth, which was fwept away towards the end of the laft century, by an uncommon flood, in that feafon when diffolving fnows, pouring down in liquid torrents from the Grampians, rend afunder the icy chains that bind the river, and dafh them with irrefiftible force againft every obftacle. After the demolition of this wooden ftructure, an army, fent by King William againft the infurgents in the north, paffed over the Tay on the ice. From the old wooden ftructure, a very unfit antagonift to the Tay, the village of Bridge-End, directly oppofite to Perth, which appears to be rifing rapidly into importance,

derives

derives its name. A causeway, still almost entire, with an arch covered with flag-stones thrown over every brook, extending from Bridge-End, connected Perth with Scone, at once a monastery and royal palace. Here the fatal marble stone, concerning which there was a prophecy, that wherever it should be found, a Scot would wear the crown, was deposited by Kenneth the Second, who is considered by the historians, if not as the first, yet as the most substantial founder of the Scottish monarchy. This stone, which, according to histories built on early tradition, was brought from Spain into Ireland, from Ireland into Argyleshire, to which, by a bold head-land it is almost united, and from Dunstaffnage, in Argyleshire, to the centre of Scotland, was carried to Westminster-Abbey by Edward I. of England, who, uniting barbarism with profound policy, laboured, by destroying or carrying away whatever might serve to awaken a proud spirit of independence, to impose the yoke of
slavery

slavery on an harrassed and humbled people. From the time of Kenneth II. about the middle of the fourteenth century, to that of James VII. the Kings of Scotland were crowned at Scone, which was also the most common place of their residence.

The Kings of Scotland, in the choice of a place of residence, naturally wished to unite, as much as possible, amenity, safety, and centrical situation. It would be difficult to find, in the whole kingdom of Scotland, a spot that unites all these advantages more happily than Scone. The greatest plain in Scotland, bounded by the greatest ridge of mountains, enhanced the magnificence of each by the light of contrast, while the Tay, rolling with impetuous majesty through fertile fields, spread far and wide below the terrace on which the palace stands, suddenly hides his head between the Hills of Moncrieff and Kinnoull. This rapid river formed a strong barrier against any sudden attack from the Picts and the English: personal safety was secured by the

the sacredness of the place; and no spot could be fixed on that was at once so secure and centrical.

Tuesday, 26th July. Leave Perth in the morning, and passing through the South Inch, ascend a gentle eminence, formed by the sloping base of the Hill of Moncrieff already mentioned, over which the great road is carried to Edinburgh, called the Cloven Craggs. Here the traveller from the south is struck with the sudden appearance of Strathmore, and the Grampians, the Tay, with the town and the bridge of Perth: and the traveller from the north, with the charming valley of Strath-Ern, through which a river of considerable magnitude, issuing from a lake of that name, about twenty-four miles distant from its junction with the Tay, meanders in a most romantic and pleasing manner. It is bounded on the south by the Ochills, green, and softly-swelling hills, under luxuriant cultivation, and covered with grass to their highest summits. Gentle acclivities rise from its northern banks, which here and there seem to discriminate Strath-Ern from Strathmore, but which sink and disappear when you ascend any eminence; so that the courses of both the Ern and the Tay are seen as one varied and vast expanse.

Strath-Ern is fuller of gentlemen's family seats, than any other district of equal extent in Scotland. The lower part of the valley, which is a continuation, as it were, of the Carse of Gowrie, from which it is separated by the Tay, is extremely fertile, and highly cultivated; and here stands Abernethy, the capital of the Picts. But the great number of gentlemen's seats with which Strath-Ern abounds, is not to be accounted for from its fertility only: for the Carse of Gowrie, and other tracts, are equally fertile, though not so well adorned with commodious and elegant mansions. The Lower Strath-Ern, commencing from a promontory of the Ochills, called Craig-Roffie, is inhabited by noblemen and gentlemen, who have part of their estates in the hilly region on the south side, or in the

less

less sheltered, as well as less beautiful plain of Strathmore, on the north. And the Upper Strath-Ern, extending from the promontory just mentioned to Loch-Ern, is not only the abode of the gentlemen whose sole property is on the spot, but also of others whose estates only touch, as it were, on Strath-Ern, and which lie, for the greatest part, backward amidst the Grampian Mountains. Amongst the delightful places of residence, enclosed in the bosom of woods, or plantations, which adorn Strath-Ern, are Lawers, on a shelf of a mountain, about four miles below Loch-Ern, the residence of Sir James, and Colonel Muir Campbell, who succeeded to the title and estates of the Earl of Laudhon. Two miles farther down the Ern, you are struck with Auchtertyre, in the midst of a natural wood, also on the side of a mountain, with the Lake or Loch of Monivaird immediately below, and the united width of Strath-Ern and Strathmore for a prospect. This is the romantic mansion of Sir William Murray,

Murray, who happily uniting philosophy with practice, has shewn the world, how much it is in the power of human art to extract a plentiful crop from a barren soil. This reflection carries our view eastward to Dollerie, the residence of the Laird of Crieff, who has also forced the cold and barren moor to wear the livery of the verdant lawn; and who, uniting a taste for literature and general improvement with the antient hospitality, and some of the antient prejudices, too, of his country, exhibits an originality of character, not less amiable than respectable. Mr. Murray of Abercarnie, on the one side of Dollerie, and Captain Drummond of Pitkellenie on the other, shew how many useful lessons, in agriculture and general improvement, may be learnt by gentlemen of the army.

On a wing of the lofty mountain of Benvoirloch, which rises by a gentle ascent from Loch-Ern, till its precipitous south-western front is seen by a spectator from Stirling Castle,

Castle, in a line with those of Ben-Lomond, Ben-more, and Ben-Leddia, stands Castle-Drummond, commanding Strathmore, as far as the eye, unoppofed by hills or banks, can reach, and down Strath-Ern and the Carfe of Gowrie, to the town of Dundee. Machany, the antient feat of the noble family of Strathallan, would have shewn to Dr. Johnfon, if he had happened to vifit it, that timber trees grow in Scotland; and that a veneration for the antient ceremonies and orders of the church, is not banished wholly from the main-land to the ifles on the western shores of Scotland. It is impoffible to pafs over the venerable beauties of Innerpaffray, fronting Castle-Drummond, in a concavity of the ferpentinizing Ern, its caftle, the antient feat of the Lords of Maderty, its chapel, public library and fchool, both eftablished for the good of the community, and carrying back the mind to the antient fituation, and the genius of Scotland. Paffing along the banks of the Ern, on the remains of a

Roman

Roman causeway, you come to Dupplin, the residence of the Earl of Kinnoull, to whose estate, according to the valued rent, the largest in Perthshire, Innerpaffray is now united. Dupplin-House is sweetly embosomed in a most extensive park, where there are more old trees than in most other places in Scotland, on a rising ground that commands the Lower Strath-Ern, and at full tide, a view of the Frith of Tay. On the opposite side of the valley, on the northern side of the Ochills, and about a mile westward, is the house, and the wood of Invermay, the subject of a fine Scotch ballad and air, through which the water of May precipitates itself in many a fantastic form, and, after intersecting a pleasant plain below, discharges itself into the Ern at the bridge of Forteviot. At Forteviot, a small village with a church, there once stood a monastery, with an hunting seat of King Malcolm Canmore's. Vestiges of the monastery were to be seen at a small eminence called the *Haly*, that is, the Holy Hill, within the memory of the present generation:

but

but palace, monastery, and the *Haly* Hill itself, are now completely swept away by the capricious sallies of the water of May, which continually changes its gravelly bed, and sports with the toils of laborious man. It would be tedious to enumerate, much more to describe, all the mansions, with adjacent pleasure ground, which run in a continued chain from the conflux of the Ern and the May, to that of the former of these rivers with the Tay, a course of ten miles, and form one spacious and beautiful enclosure. It may just be mentioned, that in this groupe we find the pleasant residences of Mr. Oliphant of Rossie, a gentleman distinguished by his skill in husbandry, and what is called the police of the country; of Lord Ruthven, of Sir Thomas Moncrieff, and of the Knights of Balmanno, now attached to the estate of Invermay. In the Lower Strath-Ern there is a famous spring of saltish water, a cathartic used with eminent success in scorbutic and other cases, called Pitkethly-Wells. The

Upper Strath-Ern, from the loch to the village of Crieff, situated on a spur of the Grampians, which advances a little into the noble expanse formed by the union of Strathmore and Strath-Ern, and which is called the Montpelier of Scotland, is resorted to, in the summer, for the purity of the air, goat-whey, and its rural charms, by people from Edinburgh, Glasgow, and other places. Woods, mountains, lakes, and the *solum siccum cum aquis fluentibus*, conspire to render this one of the most charming spots that imagination can conceive. Here the people speak both Erse and English. There is not any other place in Scotland where the Highlands and the Gallic tongue penetrate, at this day, so far into the Low Country. This valley, from its verdant appearance, is called *Erne*, or green : it was antiently a principality, or county-palatine, and the inheritance of a branch of the royal family of Scotland : and it still gives a title to a prince of the blood of England.

Where

Where the country rises by degrees from the bed of the Ern towards the roots of the Ochills, about seventeen miles from Perth, and nearly the same distance from Stirling, stands a long straggling village, called Auchterarder, once a royal burgh, but now, known chiefly as the seat of a Presbytery, distinguished by a singular union of Popish and Antinomian principles: claiming the prerogatives of a Court of Inquisition, exalting the power of the church in temporal concerns, reprobating with superlative zeal the efficacy of virtue towards future, as well as present happiness, and magnifying the importance of certain metaphysical notions in theology, which they call *acts of faith*: yet it must not be omitted, that, among that society, there are men adorned with sound knowledge, and with primitive simplicity of manners. This place seems to have lain under the curse of God ever since it was burnt by the army in 1715. The dark heath of the Moors of Orchill and Tullibardin, the naked summits of the Grampians,

pians, seen at a distance, and the frequent visitations of the Presbytery, who are eternally recommending fast days, and destroying the peace of society by prying into little slips of life, and the desolation of the place, render Auchterarder a melancholy scene, wherever you turn your eyes, except towards Perth, and the Lower Strath-Ern, of which it has a partial prospect. About a mile south and west from Auchterarder, in a den formed by the water of Ruthven, and the roots of the Ochills, in the midst of an extensive wood, stands Kincardine, the old seat of the Grahams, and the residence of the great Marquis of Montrose. Directly opposite to this, at the southern roots of the Ochills, and on a wooded peninsula, where the extremity of a sloping hill is almost surrounded by deep water-courses, in some places improved by art, stands Castle-Campbell, a seat of the Marquis of Argyll's. It was impossible that the heads of two powerful clans, living so near one another, and on opposite sides of a narrow range of hills, could be good neighbours.

bours. The Marquis of Argyll burnt the castle of the Marquis of Montrose: and the Marquis of Montrose burnt the castle of the Marquis of Argyll.

As we have thus stepped over the Ochills to Castle-Campbell, which commands a *vista* of the vale of Devon, let us relieve the gloom of Auchterarder, by a prospect of that delightful scene.

The Devon, a truly pastoral river, rises in the Aichills,* or Ochills, almost due north from its entrance into the Forth, and a very few miles, in a direct line north and south, from its mouth; though the nature of the ground has forced it to take a very circuitous course. From its source it runs in a south-easterly direction, sometimes rushing precipitately down the broken declivities of the mountains, and in others, winding gently in the bottoms between them. The scenery is,

almost

* The tradition is, that they are called *Aichills*, which is the same as *Oak-Hills*, from their being formerly covered with oaks. This tradition is probable, as their height is moderate, the soil good, and that trees, when planted there with any judgment, are sure to thrive.

almoſt every where, delightful; the verdure is luxuriant, and the variegated ground feaſts the eye at every ſtep with a novelty of proſpect. At the Yates, or Gates of Muckhart, which open a communication between Clackmannan-ſhire and Strath-Ern, it finds a paſſage, and deſcends into the vale of Devon. Here it runs in an oppoſite direction, exactly parallel to its former courſe. It glides along with an infinity of windings to the weſt, and then, bending to the ſouth, loſes itſelf in the Forth.

The vale to which the Devon gives its name, is at once fruitful and beautiful: for, though art and induſtry have not every where ſeconded nature, yet the green ſwells of the Ochills to the north, the fine meanders of the river amidſt meadows and corn-fields, the diſtant proſpect of Stirling-Caſtle to the weſt, the magnificent Forth rolling his waves on the ſouth, and the fertile Carſes of Stirling and Falkirk, covered with villages and gentlemen's ſeats, bounding the proſpect, preſent an aſſemblage both grand and pleaſant. The

Devon,

The CALDRON LINN, a Waterfall in Glen Devon, Perthshire.

Publish'd as the Act directs June 2.d 1788 by G. Robinson & Partners

Devon, in one part of the valley, has been obliged to work its way through obstructing rocks. In the lapse of ages, it has worn away the softer parts of the stone, and formed immense pits, into which the water falls with a noise and fury truly tremendous. The hollow sound which proceeds from the bottom of the chasm, and the boiling turbulence occasioned by the fall of the river upon the inequalities of the rocks, appall every spectator. Just below this, the whole river is precipitated, in one sheet, from an height of forty feet, upon huge stones, torn from the face of the rock. This fall, from the boiling appearances just mentioned, is called the *Chaldron Linn*. As objects of this kind are not to be viewed to advantage from above, it is proper to go down by the north-west side of the dell, where the descent is easy, that you may have a prospect of the cataract from below. By that way you enter a narrow glen, which seems a perfect paradise. The immense sheet of water pouring

ing from the rock, exhibiting in its upper parts all the colours of the rainbow, and appearing below, where it falls upon the rocks, like white duſt or vapour; this admirably contraſted by the dark and ſilent face of the abrupt rock, in moſt parts rugged and naked, but in ſome preſenting a few ſhrubs and pendulous trees: theſe circumſtances united, make an impreſſion on the mind of ſomething that is ſolemn and aweful; arreſt the giddy tumult of human hopes and fears, and invite to ſerious reflection, and ſublime contemplation. The oppoſite ſide of the glen is of a different character. The deſcent is gentle and eaſy, covered with green and flowery turf, ſtrewed, towards the bottom, with moſſy ſtones and fragments of rocks, from the ſides of which ſpring wildroſe buſhes, and a variety of other ſhrubs. Theſe, with the trees that grow over your head, on either ſide of the chaſm, give ſhelter to a number of birds that make the vale reſound with their ſongs. The mind is ſoon tired

tired of objects by which it is so strongly excited. The traveller quits the cataract, and strolls by the side of the river, which, in the course of 2 or 300 yards, sinks into a calm, and steals silently along its banks.

At Auchterarder we got out of the corn country, which extends the whole way from Montrose to this place, on the south side of the Great Strath, and to Crieff on the north. I do not think that England can produce, in any part of it, a larger tract of better corn. There is not any post-chaise kept at Auchterarder, although, as has already been observed, it is nearly midway between Perth and Stirling. In this part of the country, from Auchterarder to Dunblane, especially in the Ochills, they raise a good many black cattle, and a few sheep. At Blackford, as well as at Crieff, there are great annual fairs for black cattle, which are brought thither towards the end of harvest, from all parts of the Highlands, and the Western Islands of Scotland. In proportion as the country is im-

improved, this species of traffic must decay. Even now, it is for the grazier to consider, whether he might not bring his cattle to a better account, by salting or smoaking the beef, and selling the hides and tallow, than by sending them into England. The cattle yield, on an average, from 4l. 15s. to 5l. per bullock: nearly the same price as in the Highlands. The country between Auchterarder and Dunblane, where Strathmore is considerably narrowed by the mutual advances of the Grampians and the Ochills, is, for for the most part, barren, thinly inhabited, and ill cultivated. Though here and there you meet with a few clumps of ragged firs, the country is in general open and dreary. In the midst of thunder, lightning, and hard rain, the Ochills scowling on the one hand, and the horrid Grampians on the other, we passed by the northern skirts of the Sheriff-Muir, the scene of action between the King's troops in the year 1715, and those of the Pretender, under the Earl of Marr. The road

road here is the worft we met with fince we left Fort-William. Pafs through Dunblane, four miles on this fide of Stirling, in times of epifcopacy a bifhop's fee, and where there is a good library founded, in old times, like that of Innerpaffray, and, on the eftate of the fame proprietor, by a fubfcription among neighbouring gentlemen, for the inftruction and entertainment of the public. There are funds provided, both at Dunblane and Innerpaffray, for a librarian, for purchafing new books, and for maintaining the ftructure that contains them. The hall where the books are kept at Innerpaffray, is a very elegant one: but the falary allowed to the librarian is miferably fmall, and fhould certainly be augmented. In the evening of Tuefday, 26th of July, pafs through the moft beautiful and the richeft part of Strath-Allan; crofs the Forth on a large ftone bridge, and arrive at Stirling, where we ftay all night.

Stirling, July 27th. In the morning we went to view the castle. It is built on a high rock, the west side of which is at least an hundred feet perpendicular in heighth. Within the walls is the parliament-house, which is a very large room, but now nearly unroofed, and falling to ruin. The palace, also a very large place, is now turned into barracks for soldiers. The garrison, at present, consists of 100 men, and a fort-major; and about thirty-six guns are mounted on the ramparts. The Town of Stirling is built on the south-east side of the rock; the houses very old, and the streets narrow.

As the Scottish nation extended their authority southward, by their conquests over the Picts and Danes, and their inter-marriages with England, the usual places of their residence became more and more southerly also. Dunstaffanage was exchanged for Scone; Scone for Dunfermling and Falkland; Dunfermling and Falkland for Stirling; Stirling for Linlithgow and Edinburgh; and at last

last Edinburgh for London. But amidst these changes, after the establishment of the monarchy of Scotland, the natural boundaries which marked the land, confined, on the whole, the choice of a place of residence to that space which is bounded by the courses of the Forth and the Tay on the south and the north; on the west, by the rising of the country, towards the middle of the island; and on the east, by the ocean. The interposition of the Tay recommended Scone as a proper place of residence in the hottest times of war with the English. But, after an alliance had been formed between the royal families of the two kingdoms, by the marriage of Margaret, the daughter of Henry VII. of England, and James V. of Scotland; after hostilities between the two nations began to be interrupted by long intervals, and the genius of both to tend to peace and conciliation, there was not a spot in the whole extent of Scotland that so naturally invited the presence of the King and the Court, as Stirling.

ling. It is still more centrical to the island than Scone: and the sanctity of a monastery was not ill exchanged for the strength of a fortress. From the lofty battlements of Stirling-Castle, the royal eye surveyed with pride the bold out-lines of an unconquered kingdom. The Grampians, the Ochills, the Pentland-Hills, conveyed a just idea of its natural strength: the whole course of the Forth, with his tributary rivers, from their source in the Highlands, near Loch-Lomond, winding through Perth-shire, and washing the shores of Clackmannan and Fife on the north, and those of Stirling-shire, Linlithgow, and the Lothians, on the south, exhibited a pleasing prospect of its natural resources in fishing, and in a soil which, though in a rude climate, would not be ungrateful to the hand of cultivation. From this point of view also, the imagination of a Scotchman is led, by many remembrances, to recal to mind the most important vicissitudes, and scenes of action, in the history of his coun-

country. The whole extent of Strathmore, from Stirling to Stone-haven, is full of Roman camps, and military ways, a matter that has been of late well illuſtrated by the ingenuity and the induſtry of General Melville; and the wall of Agricola, a little towards the ſouth of Stirling, extends between the Forth and the Clyde. Bannockburn and Cambuſkenneth, almoſt over-hung by the caſtle, remind the ſpectator of fortunate, and Pinkie, ſeen at the diſtance of fourteen miles, excites a fainter idea of an unfortunate engagement with the Engliſh. The Hill of Largo, in Fife, calls to mind the Daniſh invaſions; and the Forth was, for ages, the well-conteſted boundary between the Scots and the Picts.

Before we leave Stirling-Caſtle, while the keen air yet blows on the ſouthward traveller with unabated force, from the northern mountains, let us take a ſhort view of the genius and character of the Caledonians. Theſe have undergone, like thoſe of other nations,

nations, the effects of that revolution and change which is incident to every thing human. But, not to carry our reviews too far back, which would involve us in hiftorical difquifition, let it fuffice, to exhibit the portrait that was given of the Scotch Highlanders by a great mafter, towards the end of the laft century, and then to add a few obfervations concerning fome circumftances omitted, and others altered, by the introduction of arts, and free government.

The celebrated Mr. Alexander Cunningham, the critic on Horace, and tutor, companion, and friend to the great John Duke of Argyll, in his Hiftory of Great Britain, from the Revolution to the Acceffion of the Houfe of Hanover, lately publifhed, a work of claffical compofition, great information, and profound views, when he comes to give an account of the infurrection headed by the Lord Vifcount *Dundee*, fays, " The King commanded Major-General " Mackay, his Lieutenant in Scotland, to march

"march his forces into the northern parts,
"againſt the Viſcount of Dundee, who had
"raiſed an army of Scotch Highlanders; a
"race of warriors, who fight by inſtinct.
"Theſe are a diſtinct people from the Low-
"landers, of different manners, and a dif-
"ferent language, of a ſtrong conſtitution
"of body, and by nature warlike. Though
"of a very ready wit, and great preſence of
"mind, they are utterly unacquainted with
"arts and diſcipline; for which reaſon they
"are leſs addicted to huſbandry and hand-
"dicrafts than to arms, in which they are
"exerciſed by daily quarrels with one ano-
"ther. They take moſt pleaſure in that
"courſe of life which was followed by their
"anceſtors. They uſe but little corn, ex-
"cept in the ſhires of Murray and Roſs.
"Their food, for the moſt part, is milk, cat-
"tle, veniſon, and fiſh; and they are much
"addicted to pillaging and hunting. Their
"children, when newly born, are plunged
"in cold water, not from any ideas of reli-

"gion, but for the purpose of giving har-
"diness and vigour to their bodies, which,
"from the continued practice of cold bath-
"ing, acquire such a degree of firmness,
"that they can live in the coldest climates,
"even in the depth of winter, without any
"other cloathing than a plaid; a garment
"so scanty, that a great part of their body
"may be seen uncovered: nor does this cir-
"cumstance, being sanctified by habit, occa-
"sion any feelings of modesty. They are
"more attached by a similarity of manners
"and dress, and the sameness of name, than
"by the ties of kindred and nature. They
"contract more firm friendships over a
"pinch of tobacco-snuff, than from any na-
"tural feelings, or instinct of blood. Their
"daily exercise, and sprightly freedom of
"living, increases both their strength and
"their stature. Their women are seldom
"married young; and are, indeed, long un-
"marriageable. They drink not so much
"wine as ale and aqua vitæ.* By this kind
"of

---

* A spirit distilled from a kind of barley.

"of liquor they fancy themselves to be made
"more vigorous; but that by French wines,
"and sweet things, men are rendered effe-
"minate. The sick among them will nei-
"ther let blood, nor suffer a physician to be
"sent for, lest their health should thereby be
"more impaired than recovered: and law-
"yers they mortally hate. Women who
"have newly lain in, wear only a loose rai-
"ment, and next to none at all. Being ge-
"nerally well-shaped, and not unhandsome,
"and of great modesty and simplicity of
"manners, though they go with their legs
"naked from the calves downward, they are
"neither subjected to the jeers nor to the dis-
"gust of the men.* Neither is it thought
"any

* In this last sentence, I have departed from the translation of Cunningham's Latin original given by the Author
of the Introduction prefixed, which not only contains bio-
graphical anecdotes of the Athor, and a view, in the true
spirit of philosophical criticism, of that publication, but
which is a very pleasing, as well as profound dissertation on
the composition and use of history in general. The words in
the Latin original of Cunningham, of which copious speci-
mens are given in an Appendix, are, "*Cum optimæ formæ
fint*

" any extraordinary honour among them,
" that their virginity is not suspected when
" they marry. They reckon nothing more
" shameful than to refuse any thing to their
" chief.* Most of them are tall, and produce

sint plerumque neque invenustæ, sed probis moribus, præter cætera, suras ad talos nudæ, nullo viri neque verborum fastidio capiuntur." This sentence has been rendered by the translator thus: " They are generally well-shaped, and not unhandsome; and, above all, of such modest behaviour, though they go with their legs naked, that they are not apt to be deceived by the enticing words of men." I should rather suppose, that there has been some wrong reading of the Latin MSS. than that this could be the meaning of the author, as it does not seem to be logical and conclusive. Having said this, it is but justice to observe at the same time, that in so long a work, which, in order to describe scenes, modes of life, customs, ideas, and opinions, so different from those of the antient Romans, and unlike any thing they were acquainted with, necessarily called in the aid of the whole compass of latinity; in the translation, I say, of such a work, it is not to be wondered at if we meet with a few slips. The translation in question is, on the whole, faithful, nervous, and perspicuous.

* The juxta position of this sentence to that immediately preceding it, reconciles the apparent inconsistencies of modest

"duce tall children, not being accuftomed to
"hard labour or difcipline, and feldom ufed
"to harfh treatment, or any kind of fubjec-
"tion. The men live to a great age, unlefs
"they chance to be cut off abruptly by an
"halter. Being, in general, poorly provided
"for, they are apt to covet other men's
"goods; nor are they taught by any laws
"to diftinguifh with great accuracy, their
"own property from that of other people's.
"They are not afhamed of the gallows:

nay,

deft behaviour, and the eafinefs with which bridegrooms take the doubtful virginity of their brides. Though far from being naturally immodeft, fuch is their veneration for their chiefs, that they deem it an honour to be, in all things fubfervient to his will. It often happens accordingly, that a young woman has borne a child to a laird, before fhe is courted by her hufband; and that child is brought up with great tendernefs, and receives an equal portion with the children of the marriage. Nor will this feem furprifing, when we refleƈt that there is fomething perfectly analogous to it in high life. A lady of fafhion is not fo much difhonoured, in the common eftimation of the world, by the embraces of a prince or king, as fhe would be by an illicit connection with an inferior or equal.

" nay, they pay a religious refpect to for-
" tunate plunderers; but whence they deriv-
" ed fuch fentiments I know not. Similar
" ideas prevail among the Neapolitans.
" Merchants who know them well, will not
" bring any goods among them, without a
" protection from their chief; to whom the
" common people adhere with the utmoft
" fidelity, and by whofe right hand they are
" wont to fwear. Their religion is taken
" partly from the Druids, partly from Pa-
" pifts, and partly from Proteftants. Nei-
" ther do they pay any long or great regard
" to borrowed rites; but carry up many fa-
" bulous ftories of their own to the higheft
" antiquity. They are much inclined to pre-
" dictions and fuperftitious omens. In
" bearing witnefs, they are not at all moved
" by the fear of God; nor do they regard an
" oath as any thing more than mere words
" and ceremony. Neither do they give
" themfelves the leaft trouble about the in-
" ftitutions of religion, until they have firft
violated

" violated it by some outrage or blood.
" They are greatly addicted to lying. Even
" in times of peace they live by rapine.
" They account it among the most scan-
" dalous crimes to desert their chief, and to
" alter their dress and way of living: for
" they think that in dress and antient cus-
" toms, there is something sacred. In war,
" they excel on foot, but are little used to
" horses, by reason of the situation of their
" country, full of dreadful woods and moun-
" tains. Their arms are a sword, dag-
" ger, and shield; and, sometimes, they
" make use of pistols. In battle, the point
" to which they bend their utmost efforts,
" and that which they are most anxious to
" carry, is the enemy's baggage. If that
" once fall into their hands, disregarding all
" discipline and oaths, and leaving their
" colours, home they run."

It is not my intention to disfigure this picture, drawn from the life by so great a master. But I cannot help observing, that

in

in this admirable sketch of the Scotch Highlanders, there is not the least mention of their passionate love and genius for music, as well as the kindred strains of moving, though simple poetry. The remote Highlanders are, at this day, as fond of poetry and music as the antient Arcadians, who, blessed with a fertile soil and genial climate, poured forth, in natural and affecting airs, the warmest emotions of the heart. The musical and poetical compositions of the Highlanders were seldom committed to writing, but handed down, from generation to generation, by oral tradition. The subjects of these were, for the most part, love, war, and the pleasures of the chace; and their general tone or style, was not sprightly and gay, but, on the contrary, sad and tragical. The first efforts of the Muses, in every country and age, are employed on melancholy themes, as being the most strongly marked by the light and shade of prosperous exchanged for adverse circumstances, and which take the

strongest

strongest hold of the heart. But the very aspect of nature, in the Highlands of Scotland, is sad: and a conflict, seldom interrupted with hostile clans, or with a harsh climate and penurious soil, deepened the general gloom. Hence, although the little wealth of the Highlands consists in cattle, rural scenes are introduced in their poetry but seldom. And, were one to form a judgment concerning the employment of the Highlanders, even from performances unquestionably modern, he would conclude that they were not so much shepherds as hunters. Their compositions, whether of music or poetry, were the natural productions, and perfectly suited to the taste of a country, where, within the memory of man, every male, without exception, was trained to arms: and where husbandry, and even pasturage, were followed no farther than necessity required. It is not long since sheep and goats, in the Highlands, were considered as below the care of a man, and reputed the

property

property of the wife, in the same manner as geese, turkies, and other poultry are in the Low Countries, and in England.

That the music and poetry of any country bears a near relation to its common pursuits, to the great objects of its hopes and fears, is illustrated in a very striking manner by those of the inhabitants of St. Kilda, whose insignificance and remote situation secure them from invasion, as their poverty and primitive equality protect them from angry feuds. When the winter store of this little commonwealth is safely deposited in a house called Tigh-a-barra, its whole members resort to this general magazine, as being the most spacious room in their dominions, where they hold a solemn assembly, and sing one of their best airs to words importing, " What " more would we have? There is store of " *cuddies* and *fayth*, of *perich* and *allachan*, laid " up for us in Tigh-a-barra." Then follows an enumeration of the other kinds of fishes that are hung up around them, to which,

which, in the course of their singing and dancing, they frequently point, with expressions of gratitude and joy.

The Reverend Mr. Macdonald, Minister of Kilmore in Argyleshire, on whose testimony these particulars are here related of the St. Kildians, received from a friend in the Isle of Skye, a St. Kilda elegy, the effusion of a young woman who had lost her husband by a fall from the rocks, when employed in catching fowls. Of this elegy, found among people in whose veracity Mr. Macdonald has entire confidence, he gives the following translation. "In yonder Soa* left I the "youth whom I loved. But lately, he "skipped and bounded from rock to rock. "Dextrous was he in making every instru- "ment the farm required, diligent in bring- "ing home my tender flock. You went, "O my love! upon yon hanging cliff, but "fear measured not thy steps! Thy foot "only slipt---you fell---never more to rise!

"Thy

---

* A small rocky island near St. Kilda.

" Thy blood ftained yon floping rock; thy
" brains lay fcattered around! All thy
" wounds gufhed at once. Floating on the
" furface of the deep, the cruel waves tore
" thee afunder. Thy mother came, her
" grey hairs uncovered with the kerch :*
" thy fifter came, we mourned together :
" thy brother came, he leffened not the cry
" of forrow. Gloomy and fad we all beheld
" thee from afar, O thou that waft the feven-
" fold bleffing of thy friends! the fhiny
" *lhonne*† of their fupport. Now, alas! my
" fhare of the birds is heard fcreaming in the
" clouds: my fhare of the eggs is already
" feized on by the ftronger party. In yon-
" der Soa left I the youth whom I loved."

The

* A fpecies of kerchief worn by married women in the Highlands and Weftern Iflands of Scotland.

† *Lhonne*, a rope of raw hides ufed in St. Kilda. It is the moft ufeful part of furniture, and a young woman poffeffed of one is reckoned well portioned. In fearching for fowls and eggs, a man or two take hold of it, and another is let down into the cliffs by the other end.

The Galic poetry now extant, was, no doubt, compofed for the moſt part by the bards who were once entertained in the families of lords and chieftains. There was alſo an order of ſtrolling rhapſodiſts, who went about the country, reciting their performances for a livelihood.

Throughout the whole of the Highlands there are, at this day, various ſongs ſung by the women to ſuitable airs, or played on muſical inſtruments, not only on occaſions of merriment and diverſion, but alſo during almoſt every kind of work which employs more than one perſon, ſuch as milking cows, watching the folds, fulling of cloth, grinding of grain with the *quern* or hand-mill, hay-making, and reaping of corn. Theſe ſongs and tunes re-animate, for a time, the drooping labourer, and make him work with redoubled ardour. In travelling through the Highlands, in the ſeaſon of autumn, the ſounds of little bands of muſic on every ſide, joined to a moſt romantic ſcenery, has a very pleaſing

pleasing effect on the mind of a stranger. There is undoubted evidence, that from the 12th to the 15th century, both inclusive, the Scots not only used, but, like their kindred Irish, excelled in playing on the harp: a species of music, in all probability of Druidical origin. But, beyond all memory or tradition, the favourite instrument of the Scotch musicians has been the bag-pipe, introduced into Scotland, at a very early period, by the Norwegians. The large bag-pipe is the instrument of the Highlanders for war, for marriage, for funeral processions, and other great occasions. They have also a smaller kind, on which dancing tunes are played. A certain species of this wind music, called *pibrachs*, rouzes the native Highlander in the same way that the sound of the trumpet does the war-horse; and even produces effects little less marvellous than those recorded of the antient music. At the battle of Quebec, in April 1760, whilst the British troops were retreating

treating in great confusion, the General complained to a field-officer of Fraser's regiment, of the bad behaviour of his corps. "Sir," answered he with some warmth, "you did very wrong in forbidding the "pipes to play this morning: nothing en- "courages Highlanders so much in a day of "action. Nay, even now they would be of "use." "Let them blow like the devil, "then," replied the General, "if it will bring "back the men." The pipes were ordered to play a favourite martial air. The Highlanders, the moment they heard the music, returned and formed with alacrity in the rear. In the late war in India, Sir Eyre Coote, after the battle of Porto Nuovo, being aware of the strong attachment of the Highlanders to their antient music, expressed his applause of their behaviour on that day, by giving them fifty pounds to buy a pair of bagpipes.*

Having thus taken the liberty to supply what seemed deficient in the account that is

given

* See Memoirs of the late War in Asia.

given of the Scotch Highlanders by the very learned and ingenious Cunningham, who knew them well, and was capable of contemplating them under a vaſt variety of views, it will be proper alſo to advert to the change which the operation of government has produced in the character of the Highlanders, ſince the period when they were deſcribed by that celebrated author.

So quick and powerful is the influence of moral cauſes in the formation of the characters of nations and men, that the Highlanders have actually undergone greater alteration in the courſe of the preſent century, than for a thouſand years before. Freedom and equal laws, by encouraging induſtry, ſecuring property, and ſubſtituting independent ſentiments and views in the room of an obſequious devotion to feudal chiefs, have redeemed the character of the Highlanders from thoſe imputations which were common to them with all nations in a ſimilar political ſituation; while what is excellent in their character,

racter, the sensibility of their nature, the hardiness of their constitutions, their warlike disposition, and their generous hospitality to strangers, remain undiminished. And, though emancipated now from the feudal yoke, they still shew a voluntary reverence to their chiefs, as well as affection to those of their own tribe and kindred: qualities which are not only very amiable and engaging in themselves, but which are connected with that character of alacrity and inviolable fidelity and resolution which their exertions in the field have justly obtained in the world.

By the feudal system, all who held *in capite*, of the crown, both in England and Scotland, and, no doubt, in other countries, were obliged to give personal attendance in parliament: and those *free tenants** comprehended not only the great nobles, but the lesser barons, among whom the king's burgesses, it is probable, were originally included. The great barons, or aristocracy, in

---

* *Liberi tenentes.*

the natural courfe of things, acquired in both the Britifh kingdoms, a decided fuperiority in the public councils. The leffer barons and burgeffes, uneafy in their fituations, as well as unable to bear the expence of repeated attendance, began to abfent themfelves from parliament. In both Scotland and England, the fovereign, that he might be enabled to counter-balance the over-bearing influence of the ariftocracy, by the attendance of at leaft a certain portion of the leffer barons and royal burgeffes, who in their collective capacity, were free tenants, exempted them from the obligation of perfonal attendance, upon condition of their fending reprefentatives to parliament. That wealth which naturally fprung from commerce and induftry, the circumftance of the parliament's being divided into two houfes, and that controul over the public purfe which, in procefs of time, refulted from both, maintained and increafed the importance of the great body of freeholders in England: but in Scotland, where

where the lesser barons and burgesses, with the great mass of the people, remained poor and dependent, and the representatives of the shires and burghs sat in the same assembly with the nobles and the clergy,* the aristocracy preserved their influence over the proceedings of parliament, and, in fact, assumed the government of the kingdom. The great baron who possessed his castle, and an extensive heritable jurisdiction, assumed the privilege of redressing every injury that was done to him, whether real or imaginary, and was the arbiter of right and wrong among his people; while the lesser proprietors, or yeomanry of the country were subjected to the will of tyrants. The amount of property which, in progress of time, became requisite in parliamentary election and representation, excluded the great body of proprietors

* In Scotland, the parliaments were ambulatory with the king, and generally held within the walls of one of his fortresses. The parliament was very often held in Stirling-Castle.

etors from that right, and created a secondary order of aristocratical chiefs, who, to the full extent of their power, imitated the tyranny of the nobles, or hereditary peers of parliament. The genius of Scotland became aristocratical throughout. The commissioners to parliament from the burghs royal were elected by the town-councils of those burghs, instead of the citizens at large. The members of those councils, too, like so many Dutch burgomasters, chose, and still chuse, their successors in office : nor, according to a late decision of the court of session, a judicatory constituted after the model of the parliaments of France, and the highest in Scotland, is there any controul on the management of those self-created *juntos*, who, at the same time that they impose what contributions they please, convert, or may convert, a public good into a private property.

About the time of the Revolution, the advent, and establishment of King William and Queen Mary on the throne, first of England, and

and afterwards of Scotland, diffused throughout the whole of Great Britain a lively sense of the rights of mankind: and Scotland in particular, as fire is inflamed by the nitrous influence of frost, glowed with the genuine enthusiasm of freedom. Mr. Fletcher of Saltoun, and other patriots whose notions of liberty were drawn from the sources of Greece and Rome, and confirmed by the auspices of the times, contended for a degree of liberty unknown even to the English constitution. This spirit of the nation, active, enterprizing, and bold, led the people of Scotland to attempt the establishment of a commercial colony on the Isthmus of Darien, the happiest situation that could be imagined for the commerce of the world: and on this bottom, a great part of the wealth of the nation was embarked. The check which this magnificent, and by no means chimerical scheme, received from the jealousies of the sister kingdom, and the remonstrances of Spain, damped the ardent spirit of the Scottish

tish nation excessively, and, by a reflux not unnatural in the humours of men, or of nations, threw them back into a languor and inoccupation, which easily submitted to that aristocratical authority and influence, to which Scotland had always been accustomed, and from which it never recovered until the abolition of those heritable jurisdictions, in which these were founded. The check which the Scots received in the affair of Darien, formed, perhaps, one link in that chain of events which led to the Union. Had the colony that was attempted at the Isthmus of Panama succeeded, the spirit of the Scottish nation would have been too high and proud to have listened to any reasonable terms of submitting to the same government with England.

It is remarkable, that it was by means of the leading men of the aristocracy, that the Union was promoted and carried into effect; although that order of men were to sacrifice to that measure, a great deal of their hereditary

ditary honours and consequence in their native country: whereas the tradesmen, and the lowest of the people, who certainly could not be any losers by sharing in the fortunes of the English, but might probably be much bettered by the change, were the first, when the articles of Union came to be debated in the Scotch parliament, who made a brisk stand for the name of liberty and sovereign power. For the very name and antiquity of the kingdom was of great weight with the people: though what remained of it, after the removal of King James VI. into England, was no more than a vain image or shadow of sovereignty: since the government, from that time, was committed to the hands of a few men, who not only preferred, for the most part, their private interests to those of the public, but who often acted according to the orders they received from strangers. But, if the colony of Darien had succeeded, the republican and popular spirit would have carried all before it.

The

The opponents of the court, in the debates on the Union, infifted, that parliament had no authority to determine concerning the alienation of the kingdom, fince power was not delegated to them from the free-holders, or tenants *in capite*, for that purpofe. The commiffioners fent into England, they alledged, were neither proper judges of this matter, nor the parliament itfelf vefted with competent authority to decide a matter of fo great importance; but that there was a right inherent in a free people, to put a ftop to the paffing of any law, as there was, formerly, in the tribunes of the Roman people. A fimilar doctrine prevails, and is eftablifhed into a firm and uncontroverted maxim, in the prefbyterian government of the church of Scotland, in which it is held, that it is not in the power of the general affembly, to fubvert or change any of the effential ufages or laws in the ecclefiaftical conftitution, without the confent of two-thirds at leaft, of the fynods and prefbyteries.

The

The court party, on the other hand, who were friends to the Union, faid, that the fupreme authority of the nation was undoubtedly vefted in the parliament; and that, "when an election was once made, neither "the tenants of the crown, or thofe who "hold of the crown in chief, nor the magi- "ftrates of the cities, had any more right "either to put a negative on the paffing of any "law, or to give a vote; but that the people "had delegated all their authority to thofe "whom they had elected to reprefent them "in parliament."

When this queftion was carried in favour of the courtiers, in parliament, the people out of doors, were every where thrown into diforder and tumult. The Duke of Queenfberry, who was the lord commiffioner, or lord lieutenant, adjourned the houfe till the next day, took his coach, and was followed with many reproaches by the people, who could hardly forbear to lay violent hands on him. During the whole of that night, tumults

were

were kept up in Edinburgh. The mob affaulted and fearched the houfe of Sir Patrick Johnftone, the provoft of that city: whom, if they had found him, they would have treated with great outrage, for no other reafon, than that he was faid to have favoured the vote in parliament for the Union. This fpirit of refiftance fpread rapidly over the whole country. Levies of armed men were made by feveral difcontented chiefs, who made no fcruple of declaring their fentiments, that the only way by which Scotchmen could now prevent the difgrace and ruin of their country, was, to march under arms to Edinburgh, and over-awe the decifions of parliament. The people of Scotland entered readily into thofe ideas and views : but the invafion of Edinburgh and the parliament was prevented by means partly accidental, and partly the refult of profound contrivance. In the firft place, the defigns of the opponents of the Union were greatly retarded by the feafon of the year, and by continual

nual and heavy rains. In the second place, an artificial channel was formed for receiving the fury of the people, by which it was, with great addrefs, diverted from its object. The Duke of Queenfberry fecretly employed Major Cunningham, an officer of very popular reputation, to raife the people in the weftern parts of Scotland, who, to the common dread of taxes, and hatred of the Englifh, added an extraordinary antipathy to bifhops, and zeal for the fafety of the Prefbyterian religion. The eyes of all men were naturally directed to the levies on foot in Airfhire, and other counties adjacent: and here the genius of Scotland feemed to make the laft ftand for retaining, within the bounds of that kingdom, the name, at leaft, and the infignia of fovereignty. But when the day came for the armed people to march to Edinburgh, where many of their heads had already affembled, their commander, with the concurrence and co-operation of different men of confequence who acted in concert

with

with the minister for Scotland, found means, on various pretences, to keep them back.

The Union was agreed to, and ratified by both nations. But this fortunate event, which prevented that general excitement which had been occasioned by the Revolution, from relapsing into the languor of tyranny, did not transfuse the free spirit of England into Scotland, at once. The Scottish barons still retained their hereditary jurisdictions undiminished, and several good families held their estates in vassalage of feudal chiefs. For example, the Macphersons and Macintoshes were the vassals of the Duke of Gordon; and Struan Robertson of the Duke of Atholl.

The private jurisdictions being reserved by the treaty of Union, it was not until the year 1747, that they were re-assumed by the crown, and the people of Scotland made partakers of English freedom. In this great event, we have a most remarkable proof and example of that principle of correction and
amend-

amendment, which is inherent in political grievances; and that abuses, carried to extremities, lead to reformation. It was their hereditary jurisdictions that enabled the heads of certain Scottish clans, in 1715 and 1745, to make those desperate attempts which signalized, at once, the subjection and the martial ardour of the poor Highlanders, in favour of the House of Stuart. Their dangerous effects became now apparent to all who were interested in the safety of the kingdom. As they were accounted private property, it was observed, that their holders might part with them for an equivalent. They were, accordingly, re-annexed to the crown: and 150,000l. bought back to the nation, that justice and freedom, which had passed away from it.

But this wise and humane political measure, great as the dangers which threatened the state from the heritable jurisdictions were, would not, perhaps, have been adopted, or even thought of, had not the administration of the British affairs been vested, at that period, in men who entertained a just reverence for the rights of mankind. The prince that filled the throne had been taught, from his earliest years, to detest political tyranny, and the noble families who had distinguished their attachment to the principles of the Revolution, and to the Hanoverian Succession, and by whose means the British nation preserved, or regained their freedom, enjoyed his confidence and his favour. In such auspicious circumstances, the opposition that was made to the resumption of the heritable jurisdictions, yielded to the recollection of recent danger, and to the genuine voice of patriotism, and a love of freedom. Had no rebellion taken place in Scotland, and our political constitution advanced another stage in that progress towards absolute monarchy, which a great philosopher, though not a great friend to freedom, has both predicted and declared to be its easiest death: in this case, it is not probable that the people of Scotland

Scotland would have been admitted to a participation of thofe privileges which, fortunately for the Britifh empire, they now enjoy. They would have been inftruments in the hands of haughty and tyrannical chiefs, as thefe again, *might* have been, in thofe of an artful and unprincipled minifter.

During the interval between the Union and the commencement of the war that was terminated by the peace of Paris, in 1763, Scotland remained in a ftate of inactivity and languor: and, as an emphatic proof that this was really the cafe, it is remarked, that there is fcarcely one good houfe to be found in that country, which was not built either before the firft, or fince the laft of thefe events. The abolition of heritable jurifdictions, the rifing fpirit of liberty, that general energy which was the natural refult of a fuccefsful and glorious war, in which the Scots, and particularly the Highlanders, had their full fhare, produced in that country as rapid a change, in the fpace of even ten years, as is to be found in the history of any nation. A spirit of adventure and exertion manifested itself, not only in arms, but in arts of every kind, both mechanical and liberal. The extreme ardour of literature and science which takes place in Scotland, has been noticed, and very happily expressed by the learned and eloquent editor of Bellendenus, a native of that country: *Scotia jam omnis in philosophia excolenda fervet, ut ita dicam, ac tumultuatur.*

Let us now descend from Stirling, a fit centre for taking a survey of Scotland, and pursue our journey to Carron, by Bannockburn, where that grand and decisive battle was fought which compleated, in 1314, the recovery of Scotland from the arms of England,

Edward II. of England, pursuing the ambitious design of his immediate predecessor on the English throne, assembled forces from all quarters, with a view of effecting, at one blow,

blow, the reduction of Scotland. "He "summoned," says Hume, "the most war-like of his vassals from Gascony: he inlisted troops from Flanders and other foreign countries: he invited over great numbers of the disorderly Irish as to a certain prey: he joined to them a body of the Welsh, who were actuated by like motives: and assembling the whole military force of England, he marched to the frontiers with an army, which, according to the Scotch writers, amounted to an hundred thousand men, but which was probably much inferior to that number.

"The army, collected by Robert, exceeded not thirty thousand combatants; but being composed of men, who had distinguished themselves by many acts of valour, who were rendered desperate by their situation, and who were enured to all the varieties of fortune, they might justly, under such a leader, be deemed formidable to the

"most

" moſt numerous and beſt appointed armies.
" The Caſtle of Stirling, which, with Ber-
" wic, was the only fortreſs in Scotland, that
" remained in the hands of the Engliſh, had
" long been beſieged by Edward Bruce: Phi-
" lip de Mowbray, the governor, after an
" obſtinate defence, was at laſt obliged to
" capitulate, and to promiſe, that, if, before
" a certain day, which was now approach-
" ing, he was not relieved, he ſhould open
" his gates to the enemy.* Robert, there-
" fore, ſenſible that here was the ground on
" which he muſt expect the Engliſh, choſe
" the field of battle with all the ſkill and
" prudence imaginable, and made the necef-
" ſary preparations for their reception. He
" poſted himſelf at Bannockburn, about two
" miles from Stirling; where he had a hill
" on his right flank, and a morafs on his
" left: and, not content with having taken
" theſe precautions to prevent his being ſur-
" rounded

* Rymer, vol. iii. 481.

" rounded by the more numerous army of
" the English; he foresaw the superior
" strength of the enemy in cavalry, and made
" provision against it.

" Having a rivulet in front, he command-
" ed deep pits to be dug along its banks,
" and sharp stakes to be planted in them;
" and he ordered the whole to be carefully
" covered over with turf.* The English ar-
" rived in sight on the evening, and a bloody
" conflict immediately ensued between two
" bodies of cavalry; where Robert, who
" was at the head of the Scots, engaged in
" single combat with Henry de Bohun, a
" gentleman of the family of Hereford; and
" at one stroke cleft his adversary to the chin
" with a battle axe, in sight of the two armies.
" The English horse fled with precipitation
" to their main body.

" The Scots, encouraged by this favour-
" able event, and glorying in the valour of
their

* T. de la More, p. 594.

" their prince, prognosticated a happy issue
" to the combat on the ensuing day: the
" English, confident in their numbers, and
" elated with past successes, longed for an
" opportunity of revenge: and the night,
" though extremely short in that season and
" in that climate, appeared tedious to the im-
" patience of the several combatants.

" Early in the morning, Edward drew out
" his army, and advanced towards the Scots.
" The Earl of Glocester, his nephew, who
" commanded the left wing of the cavalry,
" impelled by the ardour of youth, rushed
" on to attack without precaution, and fell
" among the covered pits, which had been
" prepared by Bruce for the reception of the
" enemy. This body of horse was disor-
" dered: Glocester himself was overthrown
" and slain; Sir James Douglas, who com-
" manded the Scottish cavalry, gave the ene-
" my no leisure to rally, but pushed them off
" the field with considerable loss, and pursued

"sued them in sight of their whole line of
"infantry. While the English army were
"alarmed with this unfortunate beginning
"of the action, which commonly proves de-
"cisive, they observed an army on the
"heights towards the left, which seemed to
"be marching leisurely in order to surround
"them; and they were distracted by their
"multiplied fears. This was a number of
"waggoners and sumpter boys, whom Ro-
"bert had collected; and having supplied
"them with military standards, gave them
"the appearance at a distance of a formi-
"dable body.

"The stratagem took effect: a panic seiz-
"ed the English: they threw down their
"arms and fled: they were pursued with
"great slaughter, for the space of eighty
"miles, till they reached Berwic: and the
"Scots, besides an inestimable booty, took
"many persons of quality prisoners, and
"above 400 gentlemen, whom Robert treated

"ed with great humanity, and whose ran-
"som was a new accession of wealth to the
"victorious army. The King himself nar-
"rowly escaped by taking shelter in Dunbar,
"whose gates were opened to him by the
"Earl of March; and he thence passed by
"sea to Berwic."

Thursday, July 28. Arrive at Carron, where the Carron Company have a very large foundery for casting all sorts of implements, from 42 pounders to the most trifling article for domestic use; the coal, of which they use 100 tons per diem, is all charred before it can be applied to the purpose of melting iron, as it creates a much stronger heat in that state, than when the sulphur is in it. The bellows made use of are amazingly large, and worked by water. Four cylinders of three feet diameter, are wrought by one wheel; and the united wind created by this force passes through a tube of about a foot diameter, which is conveyed to the mouth of the

the furnace. The tube is there reduced to the size of an inch and an half. It is natural to suppose, that such a quantity of air, so much compressed, must act with great violence: which indeed it does, and makes more noise than the roaring of the most violent gale of wind I ever heard. Without this very forcible engine, they could not obtain heat enough to convert the iron into a liquid mass. They have here four of those blasts. They have also the largest pump, for raising water in dry weather, when they are not sufficiently supplied otherwise, that I ever saw. It is worked by four pistons, each of which is thirty inches diameter, and raises four tons of water at each stroke, which makes about 100 tons of water in a minute. This pump is worked by steam.

They have adopted here a new method of boring guns, which is done by a horizontal, instead of a perpendicular motion, and by moving the gun instead of the instrument: but they would not let us examine it narrowly. During ting the war, 1200 people were employed here: but, since the peace, until lately, they have had but little business. I am happy to find they have now some large orders from Russia and Germany for great guns, and have occasion to employ 1000 men. To a person who has not been accustomed to sights of this sort, the place would appear like Pandemonium; for liquid iron is running into the moulds of sand in all directions; and the men, who look like devils, are driving it about in iron wheel-barrows, through every part of the foundery. At night the whole place appears in a blaze, and by the assistance of a large piece of water, which makes a fine reflection, forms an exhibition that amply rewards the pains of going to see it.

Near Carron the navigable canal from Glasgow communicates with the sea. This canal is forty miles long, and near fifty feet broad, which is a very unnecessary width, as boats of fifty tons are quite large enough for carrying on commerce by canals, and will answer every pur-

purpose better than larger vessels. The Duke of Bridgewater, who was the first projector of canals in this country, seems to have been happy enough to have attained perfection in this mode of navigation. On the Glasgow canal are a great number of locks, which must have added greatly to the expence. I think that on that part of the canal which is next to Carron there are sixteen of them in the course of two miles. About a mile and a half above Carron, the canal is carried upon a large bridge over the road. Vessels come from Glasgow to the sea on this canal, in ten hours. From the accounts I received at Glasgow, as well as at Carron, I was sorry to find the trade on the canal will not answer the expence: but I have been lately informed, that it now pays five per cent. to the proprietors.

Leave Carron, and go through Falkirk, (near which the battle was fought) to Linlithgow; a number of gentlemen's seats on each side of the road. The land well cultivated and planted: have a fine view of the

Carse of Falkirk, which is richly covered with corn.

Dine at Linlithgow, and visit the old palace, which is now a ruin. At the time of the rebellion in 1745, part of it was habitable, but in 1746 it was entirely destroyed by the king's army. This castle is famous for having given birth to Mary Queen of Scots, and the walls of the room are still remaining, in which she was born. The castle is situated on an eminence, almost surrounded by a small lake, and commands several beautiful prospects. Linlithgow is a large town, but the houses in it are not well built. From Linlithgow to Edinburgh, the country is very well cultivated, especially as you draw near to that city, and the prospect of the Firth of Forth, and the towns to the northward of it, very beautiful.

In the evening get to Edinburgh. The castle, which is the most striking object in that antient metropolis, is built on a very high rock, which is accessible only on one side, where there is a draw-

bridge. Although it was considered, before the invention of gun-powder, as impregnable, it is now incapable of any long defence. It appears formidable from its commanding situation: but it could not stand a regular siege even for a week. Upon the very top of the rock there is a large square, consisting of buildings partly new and partly antient. In the latter, they still shew the room where the unfortunate Mary was delivered of James I. A door too is pointed out to the stranger, carefully secured by bolts, and bars. The room into which this leads is said to contain the regalia of Scotland. On this subject, however, many are sceptical, as there is not any tradition of those ensigns of power having been ever seen by any person since the Union.

The new buildings consist of barracks and an armoury, as the castle of Edinburgh is, in reality, *a place d'armes* for military stores and accoutrements, to be in readiness on any emergency. The square serves as a parade

rade for the garrifon, which generally confifts of five or fix companies, fometimes more, befides a company of invalids. The eftablifhment here is as follows: a governor, a deputy-governor, a fort major, a ftore keeper, a chaplain, a mafter gunner, and three or four quarter gunners.

On a lower part of the rock towards the north a handfome building is erected. The centre is the governor's houfe: and the two wings are occupied by the governor and the fort major. From this rock runs a fteep ridge, on the eaft fide, about three quarters of a mile long. On this ridge, the old city of Edinburgh ftands, forming a very wide ftreet from the caftle to the bottom of the ridge, where it is terminated by Holyroodhoufe. On each fide of this ftreet the declivity is fo fteep, that in moft places you are obliged to defcend by fteps. The houfes being built on each fide of this ridge, accounts for their being fo very high, from ten to fourteen ftories. Choice would never have induced any

man

man to build a house on this spot, or live fourteen stories from the ground. The obvious reason of chusing so commodious a situation, was the necessity of being under cover of the guns of the castle.

In Scotland, where no marks of regular government, and very few of arts and commerce are to be traced beyond the eleventh century, and where great ferocity of manners prevailed in much later periods, it is probable that towns, and even villages were formed, for the most part, by a resort of the lower class of inhabitants to that shelter from injury and oppression which was afforded by the castles of the king and of the barons. The tenants, and retainers of powerful chiefs, in all times of turbulence and danger, would naturally take refuge under the wings of those strong holds that were the mansions of the baron to whom they belonged. The principal vassals, we may suppose, of the feudal chief would, in such times, find entertainment within the walls of the castle; while others, of inferior station, would be fain to assemble with their families and their substance, as near to them as possible. The domains, or part of the domains of the castles would naturally, in such circumstances, be parcelled out to the people. Temporary huts would be improved into houses; houses into villages; and, in the progress of population and arts, villages into towns. Our oldest boroughs, agreeably to these observations, are situated near places of strength, and the mansions of the great. They who took up their residence in such places, found it necessary for their farther security, to surround them with walls or other fences. Hence the towns or villages were termed *burgs*, and their inhabitants, *burgenses*, long before the practice of incorporating them into communities by charter was introduced, either in this island, or on the continent of Europe.

Burghers were of two sorts: inhabitants of *burgs* within the domains of sovereigns; and inhabitants of *burgs* within the territories of

powerful

powerful barons and ecclesiastics. Each burgess paid a fixed sum yearly to the king, or to the lord paramount, in whose town he lived or had his *burgagium*. Certain customs were also exacted from the burgesses by the superior, whether the king or a subject, on the sale of different commodities. In return for these exactions, the burgesses were indulged from time to time with sundry privileges, which placed them in a very different condition from the inhabitants of the country, or *rustici*, whose occupations were entirely confined to agriculture or the breed of cattle; and who, confined to the soil which they were doomed to cultivate, were not allowed to apply themselves to any kind of commerce or mechanical employment. And, for encouragement of the country-people to resort to the towns, it became a law in Scotland and England, as well as in other parts of Europe, that if the predial *slave*, or if that should be thought too strong a term, the predial labourer of any earl or baron, or other proprietor, should purchase a *burgagium* in any burg, even to the extent of only one rood, and remain therein for the space of a year and a day without being challenged by his lord, he should thenceforth be free; and enjoy all the rights and immunities of a burgess, provided that he did not belong to the king.

All these privileges, however, were found insufficient even to protect the king's burgesses against the tyranny and oppression of the great lords in their neighbourhood. A new policy was therefore introduced, of forming them into communities by royal charters, granting them a certain domain subject to a yearly quit-rent, and appointing officers to be chosen by themselves, for managing their common affairs, and settling their private disputes. This practice appears to have been introduced first in France; and, as it was a very natural expedient in itself, in all kingdoms where the feudal system was established, so it was quickly diffused by a principle of imitation throughout other European countries.

On

On each side of the ridge that forms the base of the Scotch metropolis is a very deep valley. The northern one was once filled with water, but it is now drained off, and a bridge of three arches built over the dry land, the centre arch 95 feet high. This forms a communication with the North or New Town, in which is a spacious square called St. Andrew's. The streets adjacent are very wide and handsome: many of the houses are built of free stone, and are truly magnificent. At the north end of this bridge is a very elegant building, which is intended for a register-office, and at the west end of the New Town, a ball-room, &c. is erecting, which will, perhaps, surpass in elegant magnificence, any one in Britain. The houses on the north side of the New Town command a beautiful view of the Firth, and the town of Leith. On the south side of the castle, are several public buildings. The college, in which are about one thousand students, two hospitals, which are large and well endowed, a work-houfe, and a houfe for lunatics. In this part of the city is a handfome fquare called George's. We were prefent at the laying the firft ftone of a new bridge which is to form a communication from the fouth to the centre part of the city, on a ftrait line with the bridge which is already built to the north. This is not only highly conducive to convenience, but will have a very handfome appearance. To enumerate the other public buildings which are intended to be erected in Edinburgh, would aftonifh any perfon who confiders that Edinburgh is not a commercial city.

The parliament-houfe in the old city, is about half as large as Weftminfter-hall; there the court of feffion for Scotland is held, nine of the lords always attending to do bufinefs. Under the parliament-houfe is a public library, which contains a great number of antient and modern books. Near the library the public records are kept, among which we were

were shewn the articles of Union between England and Scotland; and it is singular to observe, that those articles are included in twenty pages of folio parchment, each page containing about twenty lines only: when, at this period, twice as much parchment and writing is considered as necessary to draw up the marriage articles of a Highland laird, or to convey an acre of land from one man to another.

Holyrood-house, which is a large palace, forming a quadrangle, has a number of spacious rooms in it, and being still considered as a royal house, the suit of apartments which are intended for the king, are kept as rooms of state, but have no furniture in them. The other apartments are occupied by the Duke of Hamilton, who is keeper, and some let to other noblemen. In one of those rooms is a picture of Charles II. and his queen going to mount their horses, and a number of little spaniels about them. This picture was done by Vandyke, and

is

is inimitable. In the gallery are the portraits of all the kings of Scotland, many of them well painted; but in the laſt rebellion ſome ſoldiers who were quartered in the palace, miſchievouſly tore the canvaſs of moſt of them with their bayonets. The chapel, which joins the palace, is a handſome gothic building, and was roofed in by the preſent Earl of Dundonald's father; but the roof was made ſo heavy, that it fell down, and brought great part of the walls with it: ſince which time it has remained in ruins. In this chapel we were ſhewn by a woman, the bones of Darnly, who was a remarkably large man; with thoſe, too, of ſome of the other kings of Scotland, as ſhe called them. A human carcaſs was alſo laid before us with the fleſh dried on, and remarkably well preſerved. She called this the body of the Counteſs of Roxburgh, who had been buried there for ſeveral hundred years. This exhibition was the moſt indelicate I ever beheld: and it ought not to be ſuffered.

It

It is partly, perhaps, to the crouded and inconvenient situation of old Edinburgh, that Scotland is indebted for the new town, which may justly be considered as a national ornament. Had the Scottish metropolis been situated on an easy declivity, or a plain, however narrow and irregular its streets, the inhabitants would not have looked about for a new spot, but have contented themselves with making the most of the old, and building, without a general and comprehensive plan, according to accident or to caprice. The situation of Edinburgh did not easily admit of such improvement and extension as might correspond, in an elegant, luxurious, and enlightened age, to the ideas and the wants of a people who have their eyes open on the progressive course of science and art, and every invention that can either embellish, or add to the pleasure or comfort of life. Happily the advancement of agriculture, manufactures, and commerce, has enabled the Scottish nation to realize and

give

give bodily conſtitution and ſhape, to thoſe ideas of convenience and elegance which they naturally acquire from their inquiſitive and ſpeculative turn, and alſo from that enterprizing and wandering diſpoſition, which carries them out as adventurers, in ſo many walks of life, not only into England, and all the foreign dependencies of the Britiſh empire, but into every kingdom of note on the face of the earth. The ſpirit of adventure not only tends to introduce into North Britain new ideas or models of refinement; but it it is a ſource of wealth, as well as commerce, or rather it is itſelf, conſidered in a natural view, a ſpecies of commerce, and that of a very advantageous kind, and in which the balance of trade is wholly in its favour. A great part of the Scottiſh youth quit their country, from about fifteen to twenty years of age, and paſs through London, but without being naturalized in it, and enervated by its vices, to various countries, in purſuit of fame and fortune.

fortune. Their hearts by this time are impressed with an attachment to their kindred, their acquaintance, the companions of their youth, perhaps to objects of the tenderest vows; nay, and in some degree, to the very mountains, lakes, rivers, rocks and woods, that give a species of animation to a romantic country, and even to wild wastes which endear their native village, by excluding strangers and marking it as their own. Scotchmen, but particularly the Highlanders, are well known to be subject to that *maladie du pais*, that longing desire of revisiting their native country, which characterizes still more strongly the natives of Switzerland. Soldiers, sailors, merchants, physicians, and others, in whose imaginations, Scotland has been uniformly uppermost amidst all their peregrinations and all the vicissitudes of life, returning home with the earnings of industry and the favours of fortune, add to the general wealth of the nation. Scotland, though barren of many things, is yet *ferax virorum:*

virorum: and men undoubtedly are the moſt important articles in any country.

Nor is the ſpirit of adventure and emigration confined to the younger ſons of good families: it is general throughout all ranks and orders of ſociety. This ſpirit of adventure is connected with another ſpirit not leſs general in Scotland: a ſpirit of literature and religion, which appear, at leaſt, in the great maſs of the people, to influence and ſupport each other. In this country, the middling and lower ranks of the people are conſtant and devout in their attendance on religious duties; worſhip God in their families once, and often twice every day; and, what will appear extraordinary, many, nay moſt of them are alert diſputants in the abſtracted and metaphyſical doctrines of religion, which their chief care is to teach to their children: and this religious turn is by far the moſt ſtriking feature in the character of the Scottiſh nation.

Learning

Learning had been planted in Great-Britain by apostolical missionaries, and Roman colonies and legions, for several centuries before the Roman empire yielded to inundations of barbarians; and, retiring before the rude Saxons into Wales, Scotland, and the adjacent islands, maintained, even in such sequestered corners as Icolmkil, her sacred fire along with political independence, during the darkness of the middle ages. As far as written memorials carry back our views, we find a lettered education very general in Scotland. In every parish, the clerk, who was also precentor and school-master, was instructed not only in arithmetic and the elements of geometry and mensuration, but in the Latin, and sometimes the Greek tongue; nay, and in some instances, in that logic and casuistry which maintained their ground in the universities, and gave the *fashion* or *tone* to the polite circles of Europe for ages. It is sufficient to allude to the history of Abelard and the famous Crichton, to prove that there was a time

time when it was accounted as gentleman-like an accomplishment to be a subtle reasoner, as it is at present to excell in every thing that is connected with elegance or miltary glory. A tincture, at least, of erudition was often possessed even by rustics and mechanics, in rude and turbulent periods; and it must have been a very singular spectacle to a native of Constantinople or Rome, to behold a race of learned and religious barbarians.

The sons of mechanics and small farmers, after spending the summer and autumn in various rural occupations, go to the parish school in winter, to learn writing, arithmetic, and sometimes the Latin language: for, as to English, the boys and girls of the poorer sort of people in Scotland, are taught, for the most part, to read in the Bible even before they set their foot in a school. And a more delightful picture cannot be conceived by human imagination, than that of a young woman, in all the bloom of health and of virtue, spinning flax with her little wheel,

with

with a child leaning on her knee, with his catechifm, or fome collection or portion of the fcriptures laid on her lap: while the child reads, the work is not interrupted; for the pious mother knows what he reads, by heart.

The religious education of the Scots naturally leads them to perufe not only books connected with the Chriftian doctrines, but books on all fubjects. And, if we may be allowed to compare great things to fmall, in the fame manner that human literature was indebted in a very high degree for its prefervation, during the reign of barbarifm, and its revival in the fifteenth and fixteenth centuries, to the enquiries and difputes of religionifts; fo the religious habits of the Scots carry them forward to general reflection and inveftigation. The free and equal government of the Saxons, and a more genial climate and foil, naturally turned the bent of the Englifh nation to various purfuits of induftry, and interefted them in thofe public councils, in which they enjoyed a participation. In Scotland, the natural rigour of the climate and foil, the want of commerce and of political importance, and that ftate of vaffalage and flavery, in which the great body of the people were held by their chieftains, prefented not to the activity of their mind any grand object of hope or of exertion in this world, at leaft, within the precincts of this ifland.* They therefore looked around them to foreign nations, or forward to a country and ftate of exiftence to come. But the force of their minds was chiefly directed to the objects of religion, which confoled them under their *poverty* and civil flavery, by holding up to their views the moft tranfporting hopes beyond death and the grave, and raifing them to a fellowship and communion with the King of Kings, in whofe fight all mortals are equal. This expanded fentiment of citizenfhip and fociety with fuperior beings, this religious enthufiafm

* Being the natural enemies before the Acceffion, and until the Union, the rivals of England.

fiasm, the most powerful engine among mortals, whenever it was powerfully excited, formed a counterbalance, and subverted in Scotland all the powers of Government; and at all times, even the most tranquil, gave a firmness and dignity of conduct to the sincere professor of religious principles, which to the feudal tyrant was an object of jealousy and hatred. There are abundance of well-authenticated instances of *lairds*, a class of men who form a kind of secondary aristocracy, expressing great antipathy to certain individuals who were their tenants, and even depriving them of their possessions, for no other reason than that they were tenacious and zealous abettors of religious doctrines. The haughty chief considered religious zeal as a kind of disloyalty to himself. In fact, the grandeur of the laird was not a little diminished in the eyes of his tenants, when once they became familiar with the Jewish prophets, who treated lords, princes, and kings, as they deserved, with great freedom and severity.

But, it is not the prefent object to illuftrate the political confequences that flow from the religious turn of the Scots. Thefe indeed are fufficiently difplayed in the hiftory of both Scotland and England.—What is not fo well underftood, is, that connection which fubfifts between the literary and religious genius of the Scottifh nation, on the one part, and their fpirit of adventure and emigration on the other. Literature, of which religion is the moft important branch, is not confined in Scotland to the circle of the few : it extends to the many, and enlightens the nation. Now, wherever we trace the progrefs of knowledge and fcience, among antient or modern nations, we behold their powerful and beneficial tendency to elevate as well as enlighten the mind, to dilate the conceptions of men, to multiply their projects, and extend the fcene of their action. The Scots, in every profeffion, from books, from converfation, from the example of their relations and acquaintance, acquire a fpirit

of

of enterprize, and launch forth as needy adventurers. If they are fortunate, they return with their wealth to their native country, where they settle, and raise and perpetuate new races of travellers. This spirit of wandering will, however, abate of course, in proportion to the improvement of their own country, which, at present, appears to be in a state of rapid progression. It is observed, that arts of every kind make quicker advances in countries that have been but little cultivated, than in such as have enjoyed the blessings of skill and industry, to a certain degree, for ages. As lime, or marle, or any other manure, operates more quickly, and with greater effect on new, than on old ground, so new inventions and institutions find easier admittance, as well as a freer and more rapid course, in countries not pre-occupied by habits and customs, than in such as are possessed with a conceit, that they have already reached the highest pitch of improvement. The former are docile and active

tive: the latter prone to self-conceit, and to tread in beaten paths. For this reason, various improvements are introduced with ease and with success into Russia, which are rejected by the Italians, the Portugueze, and the Spaniards.

There is an evident, and a very important distinction, between nations in a state of advancement, and nations in a state of declination: those whom the ardour of novelty and imitation carries forward to improvement of every kind; and those who, in familiar language, consider themselves as having had their day, who feel a degree of melancholy dejection and languor; who, instead of looking forward to a career in arts and arms, have a constant retrospect to some former period in their history, and console themselves by contemplating the talents, the prowess, the splendour, and the fame of their ancestors. But the situation of Scotland appears to be, in respect to this distinction, somewhat anomalous. For, though there
be

be not in Europe a nation of higher, perhaps not of such high antiquity as Scotland, that is, a nation more early, or so early known, that has preserved to the present day its antient and original independence; nor yet any state or kingdom, now independent, that was sooner visited by literature and religion: yet it is certain, that in agriculture, commerce, and mechanical arts, the Scots, until late years, were greatly behind their southern neighbours. Scotland then, in the career of improvement, has started, in the present auspicious æra, with peculiar advantage. She looks backward with pride, yet forward with alacrity; and, with enlarged views, studies to make the most of her natural produce, and local situation.

The face of Scotland, intersected with navigable rivers, lakes, and arms of the sea, and variegated with mountains, moorlands, and fertile vallies and plains; the face of Scotland, which yields nothing to sloth, but refuses not any boon to the hand of industry, and thus provides for the health and happiness of her sons, inspired the sagacious mind of Aaron Hill, half a century ago, with a presage, that this *unripened beauty* would have her day, and even excell her sister England, whom he compared to a gay coquette. Certain it is, that the great manufacturers of England have migrated from the eastern and the southern, to the western and the northern coasts of England. The woollen manufacture was at first carried on in Kent, Sussex, and Essex. It passed into Devonshire, where it still flourishes; and has travelled from thence northward into Yorkshire. Lancashire and Warwickshire have, in like manner, become the seats of manufactures in iron and steel, which were at first carried on solely in and near the metropolis, whither they were imported from Flanders. Cheapness of labour, provisions, and fuel, regularity of manners, industry, exemption from heavy taxes: these were the circumstances which effected those vicissitudes; and the same causes

causes will continue to produce the same effects.

Human industry levels all the inequalities of nature, and even converts apparent difficulties and impossibilities, into the means of answering some useful or elegant purpose. On the bosom of the ocean, which seems destined to keep the nations asunder from each other, the busy merchant wafts home to the shores of the sterile north, the produce of more bountiful climates, which the hardiness and activity natural to cold regions convert into articles of convenience and luxurious accommodation. The world begins now to look for the produce of the mulberry and the cotton tree, to the land of thistles and sloes: and to the fierce Caledonians, for such works of fancy and taste, as were formerly expected only from Italy and Greece.---But it is time to return from this digression, to which we have been led by a prospect of the New Town of Edinburgh, a
pleasing

pleasing proof, at once, of opulence and elegant taste.

The North Loch, formerly a part of that lake which antiently surrounded Edinburgh on every side, excepting a narrow neck of land on the east, and afterwards an offensive marsh, drained, adorned with shrubbery, and subjected to a magnificent bridge, forms a striking boundary between the Old and the New Town, and adds to the beauty of both. Besides the communication that is opened across the marsh between the towns, by that magnificent structure, a terrace, which is every day enlarged, has lately been extended between them from the Lawn-Market, near the Castle-Hill. This terrace is formed by the rubbage of old houses, and the earth which is dug up in laying the foundations of new ones. That the earth and rubbage should be disposed of in this manner, was the contrivance of a very judicious and cool-headed citizen, who has borne all the honours of magistracy,

and

and is called, in honour of his name, *Provoſt Grieve's Brigg*. This, though one of the moſt ſimple, is at the ſame time, one of the moſt laſting monuments of his judgment, and concern for the public, that could be deviſed by human invention. Statues, pillars, mauſoleums, temples, palaces; all theſe ſoon moulder away through time, if they are ſpared by the antipathy of barbarian invaſion. But the ſtructure charged with the memory of the worthy provoſt, ſafely low, can never fall. Renovated and augmented, like the vegetables that adorn the face of nature, by what appears offenſive and redundant, it will flouriſh throughout ages and ages, and freſh flowers will ſpring in honour of its founder. When the proud arch, thrown over the marſh, in another part, ſhall be again levelled with the ground, as it once has been; the paſſenger ſhall paſs ſecure on Provoſt Grieve's *Brigg*, which is not to be over-turned but by ſome earthquake

quake or inundation, or other convulsion of nature.

It would be premature, did it come within the compass of our plan, if there can be said to be any plan in a collection of memorandums taken merely as they occurred, to enter into a minute description of a nascent town. Let it suffice, therefore, to say, that New Edinburgh is built, or a building, on an elevated plain, extending for many miles from east to west, with a gentle declivity on the south, where the prospect is terminated by the town and castle of the old city, and an adjacent hill rising almost perpendicularly to a great height; and on the north, and north-west, by the Firth of Forth, Fife, and the Grampians over-topping intervening hills, and raising their blue summits to the skies. The objects seen from hence are not only fitted to please and soothe the imagination, by their natural sublimity and beauty, but such as associate in the mind of a Scotchman, the most important passages in the

the hiftory of his country, and are, on that account, doubly interefting. For, without entering into the queftion ftarted by the learned and ingenuous profeffor Reid, (the father in this country of that philofophy, which is injurioufly afcribed by many to Dr. Beattie of Aberdeen) whether it be not fomething moral that is at bottom of that pleafure which we take in contemplating the grandeur and beauty of natural objects, certain it is, that where we are interefted in any fcene by moral affociations, its beauties are perceived and relifhed with double fenfibility and ardour. A traveller might behold from one of the Cordilleras, or Andes, in South America, a fpectacle ftill more extenfive and majeftic, than what is to be enjoyed from any of the mountains of Savoy. But how different the effects of thefe fublime profpects, on the mind of the cultivated European? Italy and the Mediterranean Sea, are outdone in extent and natural magnificence by Chili, and the Pacific Ocean: nor is the Po,

with

with the Plain of Lombardy, to be compared with the Rio de la Plata, or the River of the Amazons, and the regions that are extended on their fhores: but they excite not thofe ideas and correfpondent emotions that are fuggefted to the mind by the hiftory of the Egyptians, the Phœnecians, the Carthaginians, the Greeks, and the Romans.

But, at the fame time that the New Town of Edinburgh emphatically difplays the profperity of Scotland, and that profperity leads us to the Union which gave it birth, we muft acknowledge that this great political meafure, if it conferred on the people of Scotland the bleflings of free government, and extended commerce, was yet attended with many difadvantages. It deprived the Scots of the commercial privileges which were granted to them by foreign nations, particularly by France, and fubjected them, while their trade was yet ill able to bear it, to the difcouraging cuftoms and impofts which took place in England. It ftunned

and

and checked the commerce on their eastern coasts. It almost dismantled the beautiful peninsula of Fife, of that chain of towns that fringed its coasts. It drew the nobility and principal gentry to London. And so languid and melancholy was the state of Scotland, like a transplanted vegetable before it strikes its roots into the new soil, that within six or seven years after the Union, a motion was made by the Scotch peers, in the House of Lords, for its dissolution. The blood has now returned to the most northerly extremities of the empire: but its influx to the heart left them long pale and trembling.

By the Union, too, the Scotch nation must have lost not a little of their national character, and that ardour which is inspired by the presence of the sovereign, and the exclusive direction of their own affairs. If a nation is small, and inhabits a narrow country, they lose their independence, and fall under the power of some powerful neighbour. If they are very numerous, and inhabit a large and

extensive

extensive territory, they are disunited, and lose sight of their interests and honour, as one community. A few ingross the management of public affairs, and with-hold or shade from the many, the subjects of public zeal and political occupation. The greater part are thrown into a state of languor and obscurity, and suffer themselves, as is well observed by Professor Ferguson, to be governed at discretion. The Roman people lost their patriotism, when the rights of Romans were extended to the other nations of Italy.

The body of the Scotch people, it is true, rather gained political importance by the Union of their nation with England, than lost it: for, though excluded by the aristocratical sway that prevails in Scotland from parliamentary elections, by the Union they acquired wealth, which is always attended by influence and power in various shapes: and, on all public emergencies, and in all great political questions, the voice of men

men of property will always make its way, and have its effect in the assemblies of the nation.---But, what would the face of affairs have been in Scotland, if the people, as in England, had been made partakers of political power, and the antient race of their kings have still swayed the sceptre within the precincts of the kingdom? With these advantages, with a flourishing colony at Darien, and the favour of all the national enemies of England, what progress would they not have made in manufactures, arts, navigation, commerce, and all that gives power and splendour to nations? Fortunately for England, these suppositions were never realized, and both nations are happily united in one fortune and fate, as in one island.

If the New Town of Edinburgh excells the Old in beauty, elegance, and commodious as well as salubrious disposition and situation, the Old excells the New in variety, boldness, and grandeur of aspect. Both of them bear marks, and may be considered as emblematical

T   tical

tical of the ages in which they received their complexion and form. As the antient city of Edinburgh is boldly terminated by the castle, on the west side, so it is still more nobly bounded by *Salisbury Craggs*, and *Arthur's Seat* on the east: the first denominated from the Earl of Salisbury, who, in the reign of Edward III. accompanied that prince in an expedition against the Scots; the last from Arthur, the British prince, who, in the end of the sixth century, defeated the Saxons in the neighbourhood of that conspicuous place.

Arthur's Seat rises, in a manner, bold and abrupt, till its rocky summit reaches an height five hundred feet from the base. On the west side of this hill, and on the other side of a small marshy dell, lie Salisbury Craggs, which present to the city an awful front of broken and basaltic rocks. These, besides ores, spars, rock plants, and here and there, it is said, some precious stones, afford an inexhaustible supply of hard stones
for

for pavement, and other purposes; and it is from this quarry that we have a great part of those which pave the streets of London. The hand of the quarry-man has worn down a part of the Craggs into a spacious shelf, stretching about midway from their summit to their base.

From this lofty terrace, which, at all times, forms a dry walk, sheltered from the north-easterly and east winds, you look down on Edinburgh, of which, with its environs, and the adjacent country, you have a near and distinct prospect. But from the top of Arthur's Seat the view is more noble and extensive. The German Ocean, the whole course of the Forth, the distant Grampians, and a large portion of the most populous and best cultivated part of Scotland, form a landscape sublime, various, and beautiful. The silence, solitude, and rugged aspect of these neighbouring hills, with adjacent morasses and lakes, form a striking contrast with the hurry, the din, and the snug artificialness of the city;

city; while the buftle, the anxiety, and the conftraint of a city life, on the other hand, fet off, and endear the charms of thefe rural haunts, whofe genius, from the wild heights of nature, looks down with amazement at the vain cares, and with contempt, on the proudeft edifices of toiling mortals. This romantic ground, this affemblage of hills, rocks, precipices, moraffes, and lakes, was enclofed by James V. and formed into a park, belonging to the palace of Holyroodhoufe, with which it communicates. Both park and palace, with certain portions of ground adjoining to the latter, afford an afylum for infolvent debtors, who cannot complain of wanting, in this fpacious prifon, either air or exercife.

From the top of Arthur's Seat, you are entertained with the fight of a very great number of beautiful villas and gentlemen's feats. Of thefe I fhall only mention Duddingfton, the elegant manfion of the Earl of Abercorn. Arthur's Seat, on the fouth, is, in many parts, a perpendicular rock, composed of natural columns, regularly pentagonal, or hexagonal, about three feet in diameter, and from forty to fifty feet high. At the bottom of these basaltes is a lake of considerable extent, and on the other side of this lake stands Duddingston. The walks and ground about the house, which is at once a commodious habitation, and a beautiful piece of architecture, are laid out with great judgment. This villa is so situated as to be concealed from the view of Edinburgh, which, as it is not two miles from that city, shews very just taste in the noble proprietor. It would be difficult to find another villa in Europe so elegant, and at the same time so rural and romantic in its situation, so near a great city. I know not of any great city that touches, like Edinburgh, on such steep, rugged, and lofty an hill, as Arthur's Seat, except Prague, the capital of Bohemia. On the north-east side of Edinburgh lies the Calton-Hill, upon the top of which there is an observatory, half-finished. Around this hill there is a very pleasant serpentine walk, which commands a view of the whole city of Edinburgh, and all the adjacent country, which is well cultivated and enriched with wood. You have also, from this eminence, a view of Leith, the whole Firth of Forth out to the sea, the town of Preston-Pans, and many other objects.

Leith, which is between one and two miles from Edinburgh, is the sea-port of that city, and contains about ten thousand inhabitants. There is a tolerable pier at this place, with about an hundred vessels belonging to it, of different sizes, half of which, nearly, is employed in foreign, and the other half in the coasting trade. The harbour is formed by the conflux of the River Leith with the sea. The depth of the water, at the mouth of the harbour, is, at neap tides, about nine, but in high spring tides, about sixteen feet. The town of Leith, situated on the very brink of the Forth, is evidently more commodious for trade

trade than that of Edinburgh, the inhabitants of which have fallen on various expedients to deprive their neighbours of thofe advantages which are held out to them by the hand of nature.

The harbour of Leith was granted to the community of Edinburgh, by a charter from King Robert I. A. D. 1329: but the banks of the river that formed the harbour, belonged to Logan of Reftalrig, from whom the citizens were under the neceffity of purchafing the wafte ground that lay between their houfes and the river, for the purpofe of wharfs for the conveniency of fhipping. Neither could they keep fhops for the fale of bread, wine, and other articles, nor build magazines for corn, till the liberty of doing fo was purchafed from the fuperior of the ground. The citizens of Edinburgh, therefore, in order to exclude thofe of Leith from every branch of commerce, purchafed from Logan an exclufive privilege of trade in that town; of keeping ware-houfes there, and inns

inns for the reception and entertainment of ſtrangers. The inhabitants of this oppreſſed town were cheered, for a time, with the hopes of relief from royal favour, but theſe proved deluſive; and Leith continues, to this day, to be dependent on Edinburgh.

Whether from a love of popularity, or that natural benignity which ſtirs in the human breaſt towards all who are not objects of rivality and hatred, certain it is that, in every nation, ſovereign princes have uſually ſhewn marks of favour to the villages and towns where they happened to take up their reſidence. Mary of Lorraine, Queen Regent, on the eruption of thoſe outrages that marked the courſe of the Reformation in Scotland, perceived the importance of the town and harbour of Leith, which opened a ready inlet to troops from France, and afforded the means of a retreat, on any deſperate emergency, to that kingdom. In this place ſhe frequently reſided, and ſurrounded it with a wall, ſtrengthened with eight baſtions. After the

the inhabitants had purchased from Restalrig the superiority of Leith, which they did at the price of 300l. Scotch, she erected it into a borough of barony, and promised to constitute it a royal borough. But, on her death, Francis and Mary, violating the private rights of the people of Leith, sold the superiority of it to the community of Edinburgh, to whom it has since been confirmed by grants from successive sovereigns.*

Between Edinburgh and Leith, there is a small botanical garden, well stocked with plants of various kinds. It is five acres in extent: the soil, in general, light, sandy, or gravelly. Although it is not quite twenty years since it was made, the trees are so far advanced, as to afford good shelter to the tender plants. For this *seminary*, in which botanical lectures are given every day, in the summer season, the world is indebted to about 2000l. granted by the British Government, and 25l. annually from the city of Edin-

---

* Arnot's History of Edinburgh.

Edinburgh, for paying the rent of the ground. The city is undoubtedly deeply interested in every thing that may tend to attract strangers. They cannot employ the revenue of their community to better purpose, than in beautifying the town, and promoting every design that may be subservient either to utility, elegance, or advancement in science. It is but justice to the magistrates of Edinburgh, to observe, that in the promotion of these ends they are not backward.

The clear revenue of the city of Edinburgh, or that which remains after making the fixed annual payments, amounts to about 12,000l. sterling: and, it would have amounted to one-third more, nay, probably, to as much more, had it not been for the introduction of tea, and the progressive flames of that *infernal spirit*, whisky. Most of the royal boroughs of Scotland, I believe all of them, have obtained from the legislature, for defraying the expences of improvements, and institutions of public utility, a duty of two-pence

pence Scotch, that is, two-thirds of one half-penny, on the pint* of ale and beer, consumed within their royalty or jurisdiction. This duty was extended by statute in 1723, from the city of Edinburgh over the Canon-Gate, the parish of St. Cuthbert's, (which is to the Scotch metropolis, what Mary-le-bone is to London) and South and North Leith. This duty, in 1690, when levied only in the city, amounted to £. 4000 0 0

In 1724,	to	7939	16	1
1736		6101	10	8
1750		4758	18	8
1764		3550	0	0
And in 1776		2197	0	0

Since this period, I have been informed, it has

* A Scotch pint makes four English pints: but a Scotch pound is only twenty-pence. About twenty years ago, an English gentleman, at an inn in Perth, was told that claret could not be sold under three *punds*, i. e. pounds a pint. He at first swore he would have none of it: but he changed his mind when he was informed, that the Scotch pound was only twenty-pence: but that their pint contained two English quarts.

has continued to decrease, but to what precise extent I cannot determine.

The late King of Prussia was wont to say, " What have we Germans to do with tea ? In my younger days I used to take a cup of ale, even for breakfast, and I never felt myself the worse for it." The magistracy of Edinburgh will, no doubt, applaud the practice of his Prussian Majesty, and wish that their fellow-citizens had followed his example. But, the disuse of drinking ale in Scotland, which is unfortunately very general, is not so much to be lamented, on account of the public revenue of Edinburgh, as of those pernicious consequences which flow from those of the liquors substituted in its place.

Without reprobating the use of tea, an elegant, safe, and pleasing refreshment, as well as a subject of a very extensive commerce, and public revenue, there will appear to be too good ground for lamenting the general rejection of ale in North Britain, when we

reflect

reflect on its *succedaneum*, among the middling and lower ranks, *whisky*, a species of drink which is equally pernicious to health and to morals. The distilling of spirits in Scotland, has of late become a great branch of manufacture. Stills have been multiplied exceedingly: and the Scotch distillers, from the cheapness of fuel and labour, and other causes, have been able to undersell the London distillers in their own market. It has been thought proper by the legislature, to impose such taxes on the *spirit trade* of Scotland, as shall equalize it with that of the metropolis. This is certainly a departure from that anti-monopolizing spirit, which is the basis of the Commercial Treaty, the most important measure that has been taken by the present Administration. If Scotland, or any other province or division of this island, possesses peculiar advantages for carrying on any branch of manufacture or commerce, why should it not improve, and push them to their utmost extent?

extent? Not to enter into general reasoning, on a point so obvious, and to confine our views to the case in question, it may be observed, that the flourishing state of the distilleries in Scotland, promotes agriculture in Norfolk and Yorkshire, and other counties in England. But is it not to be greatly doubted whether, on an enlarged scale of politics, and of morality, which enters deeply into every sound political system, it be wisdom to suffer people in any country to convert into liquid fire, so great a proportion of that grain, which affords salubrious sustenance to man and to beast, and forms the strength of a nation by nursing up a race of healthful peasants?

The excitement that is given to agriculture by distilleries, could never be rendered either general or permanent. It is a transient and improper subject of taxation, and source of revenue which strikes at the very vitals of the people, and insensibly destroys the roots of population. From the languor of fatigue among the labouring poor,

poor, from that of inoccupation, or what is commonly called *ennui* in others, and from that difappointment and agitation of mind, whether of joy or forrow, which is incident to all the fons of men, there is fo general a propenfity to intoxication, that all wife governments ought to guard againft the increafe of fpirituous liquors, as that *Promethean* fire which is the fpring of all human calamities. Sound temperance, the parent of regular induftry, provides with eafe for all the wants of nature, or bears up with alacrity under misfortunes which cannot be avoided. The li-obvious draught, which fteeps the fenfes in forgetfulnefs for a while, expofes them afterwards to the keeneft arrows of adverfity.

But, it is faid, that the people will have fpirituous liquors at all adventures; and, that it is equally advantageous to the revenue and to agriculture, to encourage the making of home, rather than the importation of foreign fpirits. It is not, however, to be

fupsupposed, that the people of Scotland would consume as great a quantity of foreign spirits, as they do of their whisky, which, from the multiplication of stills, becomes every day more and more common. Does the native of France eat as much animal food as an Englishman ? Or an Englishman drink as much wine as a Frenchman ? I mean, not the higher, but the middling, and the lower ranks of the people. Instead of encouraging or not discouraging distilleries, it would be good policy to raise, by all means, the duty on spirits and malt, which would fall on the higher ranks and the distillers, and lower it on ale and beer, which would afford a very wholesome and nourishing beverage to the poor and the labouring people.

This commutation would contribute greatly to the health and the population of the country, and have an happy influence on the herring fisheries. The poor Scot has neither porter nor ale. The ale, as he calls it, or two-penny, which he was wont to

drink

drink before the impofition of the malt-tax, has been diluted by that grievance into a wafh, in comparifon of which, the common table-beer of England is Burton ale. Hence the general practice in Scotland, of drinking fpirits mixed fometimes with water, but oftener unmixed. This " heating potion," as is obferved by a lively writer, " is ill qualified
" to quench the thirft of a palate, fpiced,
" falted, and peppered with a Glafgow her-
" ring, an oaten cake, and an onion. In
" former days, in the golden age of Scotland,
" when men were at liberty to turn their
" barley, without reftraint, into wholefome
" ale, men of all ranks, as appears, among
" other evidences, from the poems of Cap-
" tain Hamilton, and the poet Allan Ram-
" fay, would meet together, either at home,
" or fome fnug thatched tavern, not far from
" their refpective refidences, and enjoy the
" tale or the fong in favour of Caledonia,
" or fome other difcourfe, over a cup of na-
" tive ale, and the produce of the fifhing-

"hook and net, stretched out by cheerful
"hands on their native shores. Then the
"herring fisheries flourished, and the Scot-
"tish fleets were found in every part of the
"world. But where is the salamander that
"can make a comfortable repast on a gill of
"whisky and a pickled herring?"

Without adopting this gentleman's exaggerated praises of former times, when the Scottish nation laboured under greater oppressions than even that which he complains of, I heartily join him in recommending to the society for promoting the fisheries, and the gentlemen of Scotland in general, " to
" endeavour, by all means, to pour forth
" again, throughout the parched land of
" Caledonia, the refreshing streams of good
" ale."

Although there is not any poor's tax in Scotland, there is not a people in the world, among whom real objects of compassion find readier protection and assistance than the Scots. To the honour of the lower class of people

people in Scotland, it muſt be mentioned, that they think it diſgraceful to beg, and even to accept the ſmalleſt charitable donation. They therefore, for the moſt part, purſue their different paths of induſtry, as long as they are able to crawl about, and ſubſiſt on the private bounty, however ſcanty, of their neareſt relations, rather than make their wants known to the pariſh. It is only real and clamant neceſſity that urges the humbled Scot to accept of the eleemoſynary contributions of his countrymen, which are not compulſatory, but voluntáry, being collected at the church doors on Sundays, and on other occaſions of public worſhip. The wandering beggars that are met with in Scotland, come from the Highland country, where there is not ſuch regular encouragement to induſtry as in the Lowlands, and where a failure of ſuch crops of corn as a cold and mountainous country, in ſo northerly a latitude, is fitted to produce, often drives the poor people to make a tour into the low countries, as their only refourse.

It muſt be confeſſed, at the fame time, that an Highlander, who is, from the nature of his country, and his manner of life, a more erratic animal than a Lowlander, is drawn forth to the field of mendicants by a fmaller degree of neceſſity. It is alfo to be obferved, that the fhame of begging is not fo great, when they travel among a different and diftant people, as it would be in their own parifhes. Befides all this, the Highlanders were wont to confider their Lowland neighbours, whom they confidered as interlopers, and denominated Saxons, in the light of enemies, whom it was no difhonour to deprive of their wealth, whether by rapine or folicitation. A crew of failors, thrown on diftant and inimical fhores, feel little, if any fhame in begging, or remorfe at feizing the neceſſaries and comforts of life, by whatever means he may acquire them. Somewhat of this irregular and iniquitous fentiment in morals, influences even the mutual intercourfe course of nations. A Chinese scarcely considers it as a deviation from duty, to cheat and spoil an European; and an European fancies that he is not under the same moral restraints in his dealings with Indians and Africans, that should regulate his conduct to an Englishman or a Dutchman. It may also be observed, that the shame of begging, or the sense of honour and independence, which is very strong among the very poorest ranks in Scotland, is naturally blunted by living: and being lost to the eye of their kindred and neighbours, in the magnitude of populous and extensive cities, a Scot will beg in London or Edinburgh, who would be ashamed, who durst not to do so in his native village.

About five and twenty years ago, when that excellent nobleman, the late Earl of Kinnoull, already mentioned in the course of these notes, retired from England and public life, to his paternal estate in Perthshire, he was astonished to find that there was not so much

much as one *pauper* in the parish. The collections at the church door were either sent to other parishes, or laid out at interest, as a growing fund for contingencies. Lord Kinnoull, the sole proprietor of the parish, struck with this circumstance, recommended to the kirk-session, that is, the minister and the elders, the administrators in Scotland of the voluntary parochial charities, to distribute the weekly collection among poor cottagers. Of these, however, there was not one who would accept a shilling. It was therefore put into the form of flax, which was distributed as presents among poor, but industrious women, who, even then, did not accept of it without reluctance and hesitation.

This sense of honour, among the lowest people in Scotland, is a powerful restraint on dissipation, and incentive to industry: while the provision that is made for the poor in England, by acts of parliament, encourages idleness, insolence, and debauchery, and presses down the load of taxation on the industrious

and

and sober part of the nation. The church-wardens, vestry-clerks, and other parish-officers in England, are, in general, as great nuisances, and as oppressive to the people, as the greatest beggars, to whose vices and follies they administer fuel and support from the vitals of the people. It is high time that the state of the poor and poor's rates were made an object of serious attention by the legislature.

The funds of the poor in Scotland, though small, are faithfully administered; and not one farthing is ever wasted by the kirk-sessions, on any pretence. But in England, there is nothing to be done without a feast. If the parish-officers will feast, it is reasonable at least that they should confine their bill of fare to the rate of that of the work-houses they regulate.

Cum fueris Romæ Romano vivito more.

The principal hospitals in Edinburgh are, Herriot's Hospital, Watson's Hospital, the Charity Work-house, the Infirmary, the

Merchants Hofpital, the Trades Maiden Hofpital, the Orphan Hofpital, and the Trinity Hofpital.

Herriot's Hofpital, fo called from the founder of it, a goldfmith in Edinburgh, is a magnificent fabric, which was begun to be raifed in July 1628, and was finifhed in the year 1650, at an expence of upwards of 30,000l. It was opened for the reception of the fons of burgeffes, and thirty boys admitted into it on the 11th of April, 1659. From time to time this number has been increafed, till it is now upwards of an hundred. The revenues of this hofpital amount to about 1800l. in real eftate. Here the boys are inftructed in reading, writing, arithmetick, and the Latin tongue. Their appearance is decent, and their manners are generally void of reproach. The profperous ftate, both of the boys and the funds belonging to the hofpital, is chiefly to be attributed to the truly paternal care and attention which are beftowed on its affairs by the governors.

Watfon's

Watson's Hospital was instituted for the maintenance and education of the offspring of decayed merchants, and for boys the children or grand-children of decayed merchants, in Edinburgh. The founder, George Watson, was himself descended from progenitors, who had long been merchants in that city. Upon his death, which happened in April, 1723, he bequeathed to this charity all his fortune, which consisted of 12,000l. At present upwards of sixty boys are maintained and educated in this asylum. These, as well as the youth in Herriot's Hospital, are treated with all due attention. The funds of this hospital are vested in trust with the Merchants Company of Edinburgh. This is a good, spacious and regular building, but far inferior to Herriot's, which, standing to the south-west of the castle, in a noble situation, presents to the eye of the beholder a grand appearance. It is the finest and most regular specimen which Inigo Jones, whom James

VI. of Scotland brought over from Denmark, has left us of his Gothic manner, and far exceeds any thing of that kind to be seen in England.

The Charity Work-house of Edinburgh was built A. D. 1743, the expence being defrayed by a voluntary subscription or collection made among the different societies or companies, and also among individuals in the place; and the house was opened for the reception of the poor that same year, at midsummer. The poor are employed in such pieces of labour as they are best fitted for, and are allowed two-pence out of every shilling they earn. The government of the house is vested in ninety-six persons, who meet quarterly; but its ordinary affairs are under the direction of fifteen managers, who meet weekly. There is a treasurer, chaplain, surgeon, and other officers.

The Royal Infirmary is another noble institution in Edinburgh, reared by the hand of charity, for relieving the diseases of those who

who are unable to purchase comfort and assistance. The revenues of this house, raised originally by voluntary contribution, and from time to time augmented by occasional donations, are very considerable, and the number of patients equally so. The fabric consists of a body, and two wings, all of them full three stories high; and the whole is laid out in a judicious and commodious manner. It is under admirable management, and equally contributes to the relief of the afflicted poor, and the advancement of medical knowledge.

The Merchants Maiden Hospital is a charitable foundation, established in the end of the last century by voluntary subscription, to which the Company of Merchants in Edinburgh, and Mrs. Mary Erskine, a widow-gentlewoman, lent particular assistance. It is destined for the maintenance and education of young girls, daughters of the merchant burgesses in Edinburgh. The governors were elected into a body-corporate by act of parliament, in the year 1707. At present, seventy

seventy girls or upwards, are maintained by this inftitution. The annual revenue is about 1,350l.

The Trades Maiden Hofpital is another charitable inftitution, fomewhat fimilar to that juft defcribed. The incorporations of Edinburgh, excited by the good example of the Company of Merchants, became defirous to eftablifh, for the daughters of decayed members, a fimilar foundation. Accordingly, fifty girls are maintained in this houfe. The revenues amount to about 600l. a year.

The Trinity Hofpital was founded by Mary of Gueldres, confort of King James II. and amply endowed. At the Reformation it fuffered in the common ruin of Popifh monuments: but it was again reftored by the care of the magiftrates and town-council. It was deftined for the fupport of decayed burgeffes of Edinburgh, their wives, and unmarried children not under fifty years of age. The prefent funds are a real eftate in lands and houfes, about 762l. and 5,500l. lent out in bonds at 4 per cent. The town-council of Edinburgh, ordinary and extraordinary, are governors of this hospital.

The University of Paris, founded at an early period, has been long reputed, and not improperly called the mother of all others: for, after the model of this, most of the universities in Europe were established. The first university founded in Scotland, was that of St. Andrews, A. D. 1412. The circumstances of Edinburgh not being erected into an episcopal see till long after the Reformation, and that it was unusual, if not unprecedented, to have universities erected any where but in metropolitan cities, was perhaps the reason why no college was established at Edinburgh during the times of Popery. It was not, however, destitute of seminaries of learning: in the convent of Gray Friars, instituted by James I. divinity and philosophy were taught by eminent masters, till the Reformation.

Univerſities were originally bodies corporate: and, as eccleſiaſtical corporations could hold and purchaſe property, and ſue and be ſued, not only the profeſſors, but the ſtudents alſo, were themſelves of the body-corporate; over which its diſtinguiſhed officers poſſeſſed an ample juriſdiction, extending to all civil caſes, and to ſuch criminal ones, as were not of a capital nature.

The chancellor was the ſupreme magiſtrate in moſt univerſities. This office was formerly held by the biſhop of the dioceſe, who preſided in the general councils of the univerſity, and exerciſed over it a viſitorial authority. The officer next in rank to the chancellor was the rector, choſen annually by the whole members of the univerſity.

Popery, and the inſtitutions belonging to it, whether founded for the propagation of piety and learning, or from charitable motives, fell in one common ruin. The demolition of the public edifices gratified the barbarous zeal of the reformers, and the ſpoils

of

of the revenues their avarice. On the establishment of the Reformation, the citizens, accordingly, made loud complaint of the increasing number of poor, and the ruinous state of schools. To satisfy and stop their just clamours, Queen Mary bestowed upon them all the houses belonging to any of the religious foundations in Edinburgh, with the lands, and other revenues appertaining to them, in any part of the kingdom. This grant was confirmed by James VI. who also bestowed on them the privilege of erecting schools and colleges, for the propagation of science, and of applying the funds bestowed on them by his mother, Queen Mary, to the building of houses for the accommodation of professors and students. All the grants made by James VI. in favour of the university, were ratified by parliament; and all immunities and privileges bestowed upon it, that were enjoyed by any college in the kingdom. The town-council of Edinburgh, the absolute patrons and governors of this university, cannot only

insti-

institute new professorships, and elect professors, but depose them also; the formality, but not the justice of their proceedings, being liable to review.

There never was in the University of Edinburgh an officer similar to that of Chancellor in other universities, which is commonly bestowed by the professors on some nobleman of distinction, who is a patron of letters, by way of compliment. There was, however, in the College of Edinburgh, a Rector; but that magistrate by no means enjoyed the extensive jurisdiction annexed to the office in other universities. At the Restoration, the students at the University of Edinburgh appear to have been much tainted with the fanatic principles of the covenanters: but since the reign of William, all disputes of the religious kind have ceased, and the sole object of contest and emulation is advancement in knowledge. Cherished by the munificence of her sovereign, and by the faithful care and attention of the magistrates of Edinburgh, the university has been daily becoming

coming a more extensive seminary of learning. New professorships have been instituted, as men of eminence appeared qualified to instruct youth in the different branches of science, and in the faculty of medicine. From some titular professors, without lectures or students, Edinburgh has risen to be perhaps the first medical school in Europe. The number of scholars, in the different professions, or who are studying philosophy and languages, annually resorting to this seminary of learning, have of late amounted to a thousand, of whom about four hundred are pursuing the study of medicine.

The different professors are classed into four faculties, those of theology, law, medicine, and arts.

There is also at Edinburgh a grammar-school, commonly called the High School. It has gone through many changes and revolutions; but is, at this present time, a most respectable seminary of learning. The building is extensive and good, being in length, from south to north, one hundred and twenty feet, and in breadth from thirty-six to thirty-eight, and the whole surrounded with walls.

With respect to what is of most importance in the Scotch metropolis, the state of society and manners, they may be considered under the different particulars by which they seem to be most materially influenced. These are, first, the persons that resort to it. Secondly, the courts of justice. Thirdly, the university. And Fourthly, the state of religion.

People come to Edinburgh on three different accounts: business, amusement, and education. The character of men of business, whose immediate object is gain, and the advancement of their fortune, is, in all countries, nearly the same, and varied only by personal character. It may be observed, that, as the offices of drudgery and of labour, that require not any skill, are generally performed in London by Irishmen, and Welch people of both sexes; so all such inferior departments are filled in Edinburgh by Highlanders.

landers. The rising generation acquire more enlarged views than their fathers, and strike into other paths of life: so that there is a constant influx of stout healthy men from the mountainous country into Edinburgh, as well as into other cities of note in Scotland, to supply the places of porters, barrowmen, chairmen, and such like. It is also Highlanders, chiefly, that compose the city-guard of Edinburgh. The resort of Highlanders to the Scottish metropolis is so great, that there is a chapel, where divine service is performed in the Erse language. The Highlanders naturally associate with one another, and live chiefly together, as a different people from the Lowlanders, which indeed they are. Their children are taught the Erse language, in the same manner that the children of the Jews are taught Hebrew, just as in London.

It has always been customary for genteel families in Scotland, to live a good deal in Edinburgh, not only for the pleasure of society and amusement, but for the education of their children, both males and females. This practice grows every day more and more frequent; and the fame of the univerſity, and other ſchools, the elegance and accommodation of the place, the public diverſions, and the expence of living not yet ſo high as in London, invite to Edinburgh many families of moderate fortune from the northern counties of England, to whom, beſides other circumſtances, it is not a little recommended by vicinity of ſituation. The proportion of gentlemen and ladies, to the trading and manufacturing part of the inhabitants, is, on theſe accounts, greater in Edinburgh, though it wants the advantage of a court, than in moſt other towns of equal extent in Europe.

It may appear, perhaps, doubtful, whether this proportion be increaſed or diminiſhed, by the great multitude of lawyers that reſide, and indeed, in ſome meaſure, give the tone to the manners of the Scotch metropolis. There is nothing in Edinburgh
of

of equal dignity and importance to the Court of Seſſion, nor any profeſſion ſo much followed as that of the law. The lawyers, in ſhort, are the principal people in that city; and the bar is there the grand ladder of ambition. Hence, among the young men particularly, there is a diſputatious dogmatiſm and captious petulance, which to a wellbred ſtranger appears highly diſguſting: but hence, too, a certain argumentative acuteneſs, which we no where find ſo generally diffuſed.

But this logical acuteneſs, and ſtrong paſſion for diſplaying it, is, no doubt, to be aſcribed, in part, to that ſpirit of philoſophy, which has been excited by the profeſſors of the univerſity, and certain individuals, inhabitants of Edinburgh, particularly the celebrated David Hume, ſince whoſe days every young man of education and genius is a metaphyſician. The two branches of ſcience that are ſtudied with the greateſt ardour in Edinburgh, are metaphyſics and medicine:

the firſt comprehending, or at leaſt running into moral philoſophy and logic: the ſecond, being connected with natural hiſtory and philoſophy, particularly anatomy and chemiſtry. The ſtudy of chemiſtry, raiſed to eminence and diſtinction by the iluſtrious Doctors Cullen and Black, became, ſome years ago, ſo faſhionable among the lawyers, and other gentlemen in Edinburgh, that many of them attended the chemical lectures and experiments, as regularly as the ſtudents. It was the natural ſagacity, ardour, and good ſenſe of the anatomiſt Doctor Monro, the father of the preſent Monro, that firſt brought Edinburgh into repute, as a phyſical ſchool. He has been followed by men who have improved, not only medicine, but ſcience in general: who have been an honour to their country, and to human nature.

The names of Smith, Robertſon, Black, Ferguſſon, Cullen, Monro, Gregory, and other *Edinburgenſes*, diſtinguiſhed by their writings, are well known. I ſhall only obſerve

serve here, that there are some among the professors who have not yet made a figure as authors, who by those who know them best, and are competent judges, are considered of equal rank with those who have. Mr. Dugald Stewart, professor of moral philosophy, and Mr. J. Playfair, professor of mathematics, excell in every branch of literature and science, know how to appreciate each, trace them to their first principles, and view them as connected together, and forming one whole. Such men are well fitted to raise the views of the mere mathematician and dealer in solitary and unconnected experiments to the nature and the relations of general truth or knowledge, and to temper the airy elevations of the unsubstantial metaphysician, by frequently checking him in his flights, and calling back his attention to the objects of sense, from which, or, at least, by means of which, our most abstracted ideas are originally derived.

The grand incentive to those admirable efforts that are made by the professors of Edinburgh, for the instruction of youth, and advancement of knowledge, is necessity. Their salaries are, on the whole, insignificant: they depend chiefly on the fees given by their pupils. The students here, as at the other universities in Scotland, are called upon to give an account of the lectures or lessons they receive in the public class, in the same manner that the scholars are examined at Westminster, or other schools. Thus the industry of the young gentlemen is excited by a principle of honour and ambition. In the French universities, particularly the two most celebrated, those of Paris and Douay, it is the custom for the students to give an account of the lectures of the professors in writing. This practice is excellently calculated to fix attention, to improve memory, and to strengthen the habit of reasoning, and referring, in the way of analysis, different particulars to general heads or principles.

In

In most of the classes, this might be adopted by the professors of Edinburgh, without interfering with any of those other practices by which their university has risen to its present celebrity.

As the ministers of Edinburgh are chosen by the town-council, who are inclined, for the most part, to consult the humours of the people, the clergy may be considered rather in the light of indexes, or symptoms, than as influencing, in any material degree, the sentiments and manners of their hearers. On all extraordinary occasions, however, the clergy, who are in general well respected by the people, are of consequence. Ever since the days of the *congregation*, there has been a great party in Scotland, who study to raise the ecclesiastical above the civil power, in all matters that bear the most distant relation to the church. They contend, not only that the people have a right of chusing their own spiritual pastors, but also, that to them belongs the right of disposing of those temporalities

poralities which had been affigned, in times of popery, by lay patrons, for the maintenance of the clergy, and for the falvation of both their anceftors and their pofterity. This is the grand *pomum eridos*, the main fubject of divifion in the Scottifh ecclefiaftical courts, and the *fhibboleth*, by which the zealots for what they call the rights of Chrift, try if the *root of the matter* be within their minifters. Let a man be avaricious, fevere in his manners, unjuft in his dealings; let him be malignant, earthly, fenfual, devilifh; nay, let him be gaudy in his apparel, and even gallant to the ladies, yet fhall zeal for the rights of the Chriftian people cover the multitude of all thofe fins, and raife the facred finner to the very fummit of popular promotion. On the other hand, let a candidate for an ecclefiaftical benefice be generous, affable, and juft; be he kindly affectioned, heavenly-minded, and inoffenfive in the whole of his conduct; nay, be he humble, and even flovenly in his attire, and an open rebuker, like the sect of the *Seceders*,[*] of promiscuous dancing; yet if he maintain the civil rights of lay patrons, he is not deemed a fit person to take the charge of souls.

This doctrine of the rights of the Christian people, to dispose of the patrimony of the church, is not a little dangerous to the civil government. Were the people permitted to govern the church, they would go on with their encroachments, and the days of the Covenant would be renewed. For, it is strongly impressed on the minds of all fanatics, that the *saints* alone have a right to inherit the earth: and a pretext can never be wanting for controlling the affairs of this world,

---

[*] The Seceders, who are very numerous, are religionists who broke off about fifty years ago from the communion of the church, on account of various corruptions that had crept into her, but chiefly because the established clergy maintained, or at least acquiesced in lay-patronage, and neglected to renew the covenant. The Seceders allow men to dance with men, and women to dance with women; but for men to dance with women, which they call *promiscuous* dancing, they old to be a great abomination.

world, to those who imagine themselves to be possessed of the exclusive favour of Heaven. The magistrates of boroughs in Scotland have frequent occasion to observe the strong disposition of the popular clergy to take the trouble, not only of conducting spiritual, but also temporal affairs. A magistrate of Edinburgh, reflecting on this pragmatical turn in a clergyman, said, " I ventured my " life in a storm to bring him across the " Frith, and I would now venture it, a se- " cond time, to set him back again."

During a full century, there has existed in Scotland a sect, partly religious and partly political, the members of which are vulgarly distinguished by the name of Jacobites. It exhibits a resemblance, in miniature, of that select nation, the Jews, who, buffeted and spurned by all people and languages on the face of the earth, persist inflexibly in the doctrines of their fathers. At the Revolution in 1688, King William, it is said, made an offer to the Scotch prelates, of supporting

Epis-

Episcopacy in Scotland, on condition that they would own and support his right to the crown. "*Full of heavenly stuff,*" and endued with a most "*plentiful lack*" of worldly wisdom, they refused to close with his proposal. Presbytery, of course, was established, and all of the Episcopal persuasion degraded to the rank of sectaries, in which they have since remained.

For sixty years after this period, they formed a strong and respectable party in the north; frequent attempts to restore the exiled Stuarts, supporting their spirits, and inspiring them with hopes of once more gaining the mastery. The romantic and most ruinous adventure of Charles Edward, in 1745, gave the finishing blow to their political importance. Even as a religious society, they have been terribly lopped and thinned, by the introduction of certain religious adventurers, called Qualified Episcopal Clergymen, though very unjustly, as belonging to no bishopric.

Yet

Yet even thus extenuated, and verging swiftly towards annihilation, they preserve, with no small self-importance and fanciful dignity, the form of a national church. Though they "do not now thunder in the capitol, they hold their little senate at Utica, and rail at *Cæsar*." Their bishops are chosen and consecrated, if not with all the pride, pomp, and circumstance of glorious prelacy; at least with the imitation thereof; and the election of a Pope is not attended with more intrigue and cabal. Those venerable fathers lately stept forth a little to the public view, by imparting a portion of their apostolic authority to Doctor Seabury, an American clergyman. One of them, on that occasion, published a sermon, which, in the present period of liberality and extended science, must appear as a curious remain of that sectarian spirit which prevailed in the last century. They find great consolation in likening their state to that of the primitive church, unconnected with political society, and independent

pendent of the powers of this world; and though the resembling features between these be indeed very few and faint, yet uninformed and credulous minds readily discover a similitude, and the preachers, who by that craft have their living, fail not to illustrate and enforce the doctrine. Whether such a metaphysical source of comfort will long preserve the party in existence, can only be matter of conjecture. To determine the progress and periods of religious opinion, philosophy exerts her powers in vain.

It may not, perhaps, be thought very characteristical of Edinburgh to observe, that there is a variety of clubs among the men in which hard drinking is still kept up, though not to such excess as formerly; and that the women, especially the younger ones, are not so attentive to domestic matters, as their grand-mothers, and much given to strolling in the streets.

The people of Edinburgh, as well as the Scotch nation in general, are commonly said to poſſeſs great preſence of mind, as well as great reſolution in ſituations of difficulty and danger. Even tumultuous aſſemblies, or mobs, it is remarked, have often conducted their deſigns with great deliberation, as well as perſeverance. A ſtriking example of this occurred in 1736, in the murder of Captain Porteous, commandant of the city-guard. The popular diſcontents with the Union were not allayed, when the impoſition of new taxes, particularly the malt-tax, excited throughout Scotland a general diſſatisfaction, and almoſt a ſpirit of oppoſition to Government. The new taxes were to be enforced, and the authority of the legiſlature maintained, by the execution of a daring ſmuggler who had ſignalized his boldneſs in ſetting the laws at defiance. Orders were given to Captain Porteous to employ, if neceſſary, the force committed to his care, in quelling a threatened inſurrection in favour of the condemned priſoner. A ſhower of ſtones, broken glaſſes, and other miſſile weapons diſcharged

charged againſt the officers of juſtice, at the common place of execution, in the Graſs-Market, announced the premeditated and predicted onſet. The ſoldiers having repeatedly fired their pieces, charged only with powder, to no purpoſe, the Captain of the guard ordered them at laſt to charge with bullet. Six men of the mob were killed, and about double of that number wounded. The Captain, proſecuted by the City of Edinburgh, and condemned by a jury of enraged citizens to death, being naturally conſidered as a ſufferer in the cauſe of Government, obtained a reprieve from Queen Caroline, who was at the head of the Regency, during the abſence of George II. her royal conſort, in his paternal dominions in Germany.

But the Edinburghers, fired with national jealouſy and reſentment, conſidered the royal exerciſe of mercy as an inſult to the dignity of the Scottiſh metropolis, and an injury to the *manes* of the ſlain. An armed rabble, on the night before the day fixed for the execution of Porteous, ſurprized

prized and difarmed the town-guard, feized the gates of the city for preventing the admiffion of the troops quartered in the fuburbs, fet fire to the prifon doors, and fetting loofe the other prifoners, dragged Captain Porteous to the Grafs-Market, hung him up on a dyer's poft, and difperfed themfelves, in perfect tranquillity, to their refpective places of refidence.

The principal authors of this enormous outrage were concealed from the vengeful enquiries of Government, by the favour of their fellow-citizens; and even they who were moft operative in carrying the threats of the populace into execution, found, for a while, that countenance from thofe who were affociated with them in purpofe, though not in actions, which all partakers in guilt are wont to fhew to one another, while the fury that urged them to the commiffion of crimes remains unabated. But the tide of popular rage fubfided, with the hoftile fearches of Government, and Captain Porteous began

to

to appear in the light of an unfortunate officer, who, considering himself under an obligation to support the officers of justice, and to save his men from the increasing and alarming fury of the multitude, yielded with reluctance to the necessity of preventing the effects of confirmed revolt and rebellion, by a timely example of that danger which attended an open resistance of established government. The rash men who *did the deed,* excluded from the sympathy and approbation of their former abettors, proved how natural it is for mankind to judge of themselves, according to the opinions entertained of them by others, and by what powerful bands the Father of mankind has restrained them from the shedding of blood. They now felt a degree of shame and remorse, and sought to escape the eyes of their acquaintance, by travelling into foreign parts, or in the obscurity of the English metropolis. Some of these unhappy men, with their own hands, put an end to their existence, and others took shelter,

shelter, where they ought, in repentance and religious devotion. But he, who performed the last office of the executioner, endeavoured, with various success, to brave the rebukes of the judge within, by associating with buffoons and vagabonds, who, by a smattering of learning, and common-place sophisms and jokes, endeavoured to confound all distinctions between vice and virtue. He was submissive even to abject humiliation to his superiors; but gave vent to the natural turbulence of his mind in insolence towards the poor and helpless. Having daringly violated the laws of society, he attached himself chiefly to a man who, at one period of his life, it is said, had exercised the vocation of a robber; and he was observed to delight, on all occasions, in fomenting discord, aggravating what was gloomy, and predicting what was dreadful. In his gait he was sometimes quick, sometimes slow. Now he would give vent to the inward storm that raged in his breast, by bellowing with great vociferation against any

person

person he deemed either not capable, or not inclined to retort his abuse: and now he would be sunk in profound melancholy and silence. His manner, in short, was unequal and violent; and there was something in his countenance, during the whole course of his life, which, had one been searching for an executioner amongst a thousand bye-standers, would have said, at once, there is the man!

Such are the observations that have been made on the character and the fate of the men who were most actively concerned in the murder of Captain Porteous; whose story, though not so interesting as that of those who have assassinated princes and kings, is yet, in a moral view, equally instructive: since it shews that there is no change of situation or place, that not the *civium ardor prava jubentium*, nor all the opiates of either sceptical or convivial society, can secure the man who has unfortunately been guilty of blood, from the stings of conscience, that impartial reviewer, and inexorable judge of human thoughts, words, and actions.---Having spent a week at Edinburgh, where we were entertained with great elegance, as well as hospitality, we leave it on

Friday, the 5th of August, and go to Kelso. Pass through Dalkeith, where the Duke of Buccleugh has an elegant seat, and where there is a great deal of fine old timber. This being a very bad day, we had very little opportunity of seeing the country round us. As far as I could discern, the land, for eight miles from Edinburgh, seems to be well cultivated. Beyond this distance, for a course of twenty-five miles, till you get near Kelso, the country around is mountainous, barren, and thinly inhabited.

Kelso is, without exception, the most beautiful spot I have seen in Scotland. It is a well-built little town, situated on the banks of the Tweed, over which is an elegant bridge, just below the conflux of the Teviot and the Tweed. From this bridge there is a most beautiful view of the town, the Duke of Roxburgh's elegant house, called Fleurs, those of Sir James Duglass, Sir James Pringle,

gle, Mr. Davison, and several other modern mansions. The country is well wooded, and highly improved. This scene is considerably enriched by the ruins of the old abbey, built by David I. The distant hills, particularly the Elder-Hills, are taken into the view, and, on the whole, as compleat a prospect is furnished as I ever saw.

But, this is a miniature picture. For, a space of two miles either way from this spot, brings you into an open country again; not indeed without its beauties, but too naked for the imagination: however, much pains have been taken lately to cultivate this part of the country, which produces a great quantity of corn; many inclosures are also made of thorn, but those hedges are not yet grown high enough to afford shelter. Here also are numerous plantations, though only in an infant state. In time, I see nothing to prevent the banks of the Tweed from becoming as beautiful as the banks of the Thames.

Thursday, the 11th of August. Leave Kelso, and ride by the side of the Tweed to

Coldstream; cross an elegant bridge of five arches, and enter England: and here it is well worthy of remark, that all the bridges in Scotland are built with much more taste and elegance, than any in England. The stone of which they are generally constructed is of a brown colour, and appears to be very durable: indeed the latter quality seems to be absolutely necessary, for all the rivers in Scotland, as in all mountainous countries, are subject to great floods, and run with violent rapidity, insomuch that some of the bridges have circular openings between each arch, to discharge the water when the arches are full.

Pass Flouden Field. As I have given an account from Mr. Hume, of a celebrated engagement, in which the English were defeated, with great slaughter, by the Scots; so I shall here, to shew my impartiality, take occasion to introduce, from the same author, an action not less famous, in which the Scots were routed, with still heavier loss, by the English.

" The

"The King of Scotland, (James IV.) had
"assembled the whole force of his kingdom;
"and having passed the Tweed with a brave,
"though a tumultuary army of about
"50,000 men, he ravaged those parts of
"Northumberland which lay nearest that
"river, and he employed himself in taking
"the castles of Norham, Etal, Werke, Ford,
"and other places of little importance. Lady
"Ford, being taken prisoner in her castle,
"was presented to James, and so gained on
"the affections of that prince, that he wasted
"in pleasure the critical time, which, during
"the absence of his enemy, he should have
"employed in pushing his conquests. His
"troops, lying in a barren country, where
"they soon consumed all the provisions, be-
"gan to be pinched with hunger: and as
"the authority of the prince was feeble, and
"military discipline, during that age, ex-
"tremely relaxed, many of them had stolen
"from the camp, and retired homewards.
"Meanwhile, the Earl of Surrey, having
"collected

" collected a force of 26,000 men, of which
" 5,000 had been sent over from the king's
" army in France, marched to the defence of
" the country, and approached the Scots,
" who lay on some high ground near the
" Hills of Cheviot. The River Till ran be-
" tween the armies, and prevented an en-
" gagement: Surrey therefore sent a herald
" to the Scotch camp, challenging the enemy
" to descend into the plain of Millfield, which
" lay towards the south; and there, ap-
" pointing a day for the combat, to try their
" valour on equal ground. As he received
" no satisfactory answer, he made a feint
" of marching towards Berwic; as if he
" intended to enter into Scotland, to lay
" waste the borders, and cut off the provi-
" sions of the enemy. The Scotch army, in
" order to prevent his purpose, put them-
" selves in motion; and having set fire to the
" huts in which they had quartered, they
" descended from the hills. Surrey, taking
" advantage of the smoke, which was blown
" towards

"towards him, and which concealed his
"movements, paffed the Till with his artil-
"lery and vanguard at the bridge of Twifel,
"and fent the reft of his army to feek a ford
"higher up the river.

"An engagement was now become inevi-
"table, and both fides prepared for it with
"tranquillity and order. The Englifh di-
"vided their army into two lines : Lord
"Howard led the main body of the firft line,
"Sir Edmond Howard the right wing, Sir
"Marmaduke Conftable the left. The Earl
"of Surrey himfelf commanded the main
"body of the fecond line, Lord Dacres the
"right wing, Sir Edward Stanley the left.
"The front of the Scots prefented three di-
"vifions to the enemy : the middle was led
"by the King himfelf: the right by the Earl
"of Huntley, affifted by Lord Hume : the
"left by the Earls of Lenox and Argyle. A
"fourth divifion under the Earl of Bothwel
"made a body of referve. Huntley began
"the battle ; and after a fharp conflict, put

" to flight the left wing of the English, and
" chaced them off the field: but on return-
" ing from the pursuit, he found the whole
" Scottish army in great disorder. The di-
" vision under Lenox and Argyle, elated with
" the success of the other wing, had broken
" their ranks, and notwithstanding the re-
" monstrances and entreaties of La Motte,
" the French ambassador, had rushed head-
" long upon the enemy. Not only Sir Ed-
" mond Howard, at the head of his division,
" received them with great valour; but
" Dacres, who commanded in the second line,
" wheeling about during the action, fell upon
" their rear, and put them to the sword with-
" out resistance. The division under James
" and that under Bothwel, animated by the
" valour of their leaders, still made head
" against the English, and throwing them-
" selves into a circle, protracted the action,
" till night separated the combatants. The
" victory seemed yet uncertain, and the num-
" bers, that fell on each side, were nearly
" equal,

"equal, amounting to above 5,000 men: but
"the morning difcovered where the advan-
"tage lay. The Englifh had loft only per-
"fons of fmall note; but the flower of the
"Scottifh nobility had fallen in battle, and
"their king himfelf, after the moft diligent
"enquiry, could no where be found. In
"fearching the field, the Englifh met with
"a dead body, which refembled him, and
"was arrayed in a fimilar habit; and they
"put it in a leaden coffin, and fent it to
"London. During fome time it was kept
"unburied; becaufe James died under fen-
"tence of excommunication, on account of
"his confederacy with France, and his op-
"pofition to the holy fee. But upon Hen-
"ry's application, who pretended that that
"prince had, in the inftant before his death,
"difcovered figns of repentance, abfolution
"was given him, and his body was interred.
"The Scots, however, ftill afferted, that it
"was not James's body, which was found
"on the field of battle, but that of one El-
             "phinfton,

" phinston, who had been arrayed in arms
" resembling their king's, in order to divide
" the attention of the English, and share the
" danger with his master. It was believed
" that James had been seen crossing the
" Tweed at Kelso; and some imagined that
" he had been killed by the vassals of Lord
" Hume, whom that nobleman had insti-
" gated to commit so enormous a crime.
" But the populace entertained the opinion
" that he was still alive, and having secretly
" gone in pilgrimage to the holy land, would
" soon return, and take possession of the
" throne. This fond conceit was long en-
" tertained among the Scots."

The musical genius of Scotland expressed the moans of the nation in the deeply plaintive notes of *The Flowers of the Forest*. On the battle of Flouden, another ballad was also composed, of another strain, in praise of the *souters* (shoe-makers) of Selkirk, and in ridicule of the Earl of Hume. When the Scottish army advanced southward towards the

the borders of England, a band of eighty *souters* joined the royal army, under the conduct of the town-clerk of Selkirk. They fought with great bravery, and were mostly cut off. A few who escaped, found, on their return, in the forest of Lady-Wood-Edge, the wife of one of their brethren, lying dead, and her child sucking her breast. The Town of Selkirk, from this circumstance, obtained for their arms, a woman sitting upon a sarcophagus, holding a child in her arms; in the back ground, a wood; and, on the sarcophagus, the arms of Scotland.

Millfield Plain, where the battle of Flouden was fought, extends about five miles each way, and is entirely surrounded by barren mountains, the Cheviot Hills forming the southern boundary. Pass on to Wollerhaugh-head, a small poor town: from Woller to Alnwick, the road goes round the Cheviot Hills, through a wild and uncultivated country.

At

At Alnwick is the Duke of Northumberland's Caftle, a very large pile of building, in the fhape of an octagon, the inner court forming a circle. In this part of the caftle are the rooms for ftate and bed-chambers. The library is a large and elegant apartment, and the chapel adjoining to it is fitted up entirely in the Gothic ftile, an humble —imitation of that order of architecture. The chapel is lighted by a large window, painted with great tafte: all the rooms in the caftle, three of which are very fpacious and elegant, are, like the chapel, fitted in the Gothic ftile. The fervants apartments, and all the offices, are diftinct from the caftle, but all in the fame ftile of architecture. On the battlements are a great number of ftatues of warriors, in various attitudes of defence, apparently as large as life, which makes it appear as if an enemy was ftorming it. On the right of the inner gateway, is ftill to be feen a dungeon, with an

iron

iron grate, the Gothic emblem of lawlefs will and arbitrary power.

The grounds round Alnwick are very extenfive, reaching all the way to the fea, but moft of the improvements are modern. Great part of the caftle has been built, or rebuilt by the prefent Duke. All the plantations are very young: none of the trees feem to bear the appearance of more than forty years.

The town of Alnwick is not very extenfive, but neat, and well built: fome of the houfes are very antient, others modern and elegant. The eaft and weft gates are very antient, and towards the north, the Duke has lately built an elegant gate-way, with a handfome tower upon it, in the Gothic ftile. This tower was intended to have bells placed in it, but the ftructure was found to be too flight. The church is a fpacious and elegant building.

Were the Dukes of Northumberland, in thefe peaceable times, like their neighbour the Duke of Bridgewater, to exercife the fame ardour in the promotion of arts and commerce, which their anceftors, in turbulent times, difplayed in arms, Alnwick and the adjacent country might be rendered as famous for manufactures as it was formerly renowned for bloody battles. There is not in any part of Britain, better wool than that which is produced in the hilly tracts in the fouth of Scotland, and the north of England. This circumftance, with abundance of fuel, and vicinity to the fea, is fufficient to prove this pofition.

In the times of the Heptarchy, before the different kingdoms of which England originally confifted, were united in one,* that of Northumberland extended from the Tweed to the Humber, and comprehended, befides the county of that name, Cumberland, Weftmoreland, the whole of Yorkfhire, Lancafhire,

---

* It is remarkable, that, at this moment, the Ifland of Madagafcar is divided into feven diftinct kingdoms, each governed by its own king, who enjoys his authority and title by inheritance.

Lancashire, and the Bishoprick of Durham. The capital of this kingdom was York, a town equally famous during the Roman, the Saxon, and the Norman æra. It is from this last period that we are enabled to account for some customs that prevail among the inhabitants, and for that particular dialect, which distinguishes a Yorkshireman and Northumbrian, including under that name the inhabitants of Westmoreland and Cumberland, from all others in this kingdom.

It is well known, that the antient kingdom of Northumberland was, for ages, the grand subject of contention between the Saxons and the Danes, and when these were at length expelled from England, between the Saxons and the Norwegians. The first Danish expedition of which we have any certain account, was made by King Reynar Lodbrok, a prince equally imprudent and unfortunate. He was slain by Ella king of Northumberland; who in his turn was slain by the sons of Reynar, and was succeeded by Ivar the Dane, who fixed his refidence at York. On the death of Ivar, the kingdom of Northumberland returned to the obedience of her former lords, the kings of the Saxons. At length King Athelftan gave it to Eric, who had been expelled from his kingdom of Norway, fon of Harold the fair-haired, appointing him guardian of the northern coafts, againft the incurfions of the Norwegians.

It was in the time of Eric that the famous battle of Brunanburgh was fought by King Athelftan, againft Conftantine king of Scotland, and Olave, one of the kings of Ireland. Athelftan received from his Norwegian allies the moft powerful fupport on all occafions of danger. The Norwegians, in the intereft and fervice of King Athelftan were joined by Egitt and Thorolf, two chiefs from Iceland. Thorolf was killed, but Egitt, loaded with the moft ample tokens of the royal favour of Athelftan, returned to his native country. Nor were thefe the only Icelandic adventurers who vifited England, and paid their homage

mage to her kings. It was a cuſtom among the Icelanders to travel as ſoldiers of fortune into foreign countries; to enquire into the conſtitution and manners of the nations among whom they ſojourned; and to report, on their return home, whatever they deemed likely to improve the government of Iceland. And hence, the laws of Iceland, framed during the time of the republic, contain or refer to many particulars that throw not a little light on our own. Trial by jury, for example, was adhered to in Iceland, with ſtill greater care than in England; the nature of juries more fully diſplayed; and the duty of jurymen more exactly defined. In Iceland, the number of men of which juries conſiſted, varied from ſix or ſeven even to an hundred, according to the magnitude of the crime to be tried; and it was always in the power of the perſon accuſed, to challenge not only any part, but even the whole of the jury: ſo great was the regard formerly paid in that remote ifland to the natural rights of mankind!

There is not, in the prefent period, any court in Europe, the Ruffian not excepted, which expends fuch large fums on the advancement of arts and fciences as that of Denmark. His Danifh Majefty, the Prince Royal, and the great men who conduct the affairs of the kingdom, ftrongly impreffed with the juft notion that great light may be thrown on the prefent ftate of Denmark, as well as of other kingdoms, by an accurate enquiry into the fettlements or colonies of their anceftors, have given orders for publifhing a collection of all the Danifh Writers of the middle age.* For this purpofe, the learned Jacob Langebeck was fent, at his Majefty's expence, on a tour through

---

* Of the *Scriptores Rerum Danicarum*, fix volumes in folio are already printed; among which is a work by Snorro Thurlfon, publifhed at the expence of his Royal Highnefs Prince Frederick, brother to the King, which illuftrates tho antient hiftory of Northumberland.

through Sweden, and along the shores of the Baltic; and for the same end, Grim Johnson Thorkelyn, L.L.D. Professor of Antiquities of the University of Copenhagen, and Keeper of the Privy Archives, is, at the time of writing this, in England. This gentleman, a native of Iceland, who was bred to the profession of the law, has deservedly gained the favour of his royal master; and, by the works which he has already published, an established fame. It is to be hoped, that he will give us a critical account of many of our English customs, into which, in the course of his tour, he has made very judicious enquiries. His account of the Danish invasion of Northumberland is ready for being printed; and he is, at present, engaged in preparing for the press an English translation of the Laws of the Republic of Iceland, with proper illustrations, which will undoubtedly afford much rational entertainment to the antiquarian and the philosopher;

and, perhaps, some useful hints to legislators and statesmen.

Of the Danish and Norwegian remains in the antient kingdom of Northumberland, we have a very striking instance, in the extraordinary care and attachment of the Northumbrians and Yorkshiremen to their horses. The Norwegians and Icelanders treat their horses not only with the utmost care, but with a degree of affection. It was in conformity to the genius of his countrymen, that John Erischen, an Icelandic gentleman, wrote a Treatise de *Philippia Veterum*,* printed at Copenhagen, 1757.

The following are examples of words, the same in the Norwegian and Icelandic language; and in that of the low countries in Scotland, and the northern counties in England.

A *gait*, a foot path, or road.
An *ark*, a large chest.
Aud, old.

A *bairn*,

---

* The love of the antients for their horses.

A *bairn*, a child.
Beeting with child---*i. e.* gravid.
Blake, yellow, pale.
Capel, a horse, a working horse.
Elden, fuel for fire.
To *elt*, to knead.
To *feal*, to hide.
A *frith*, an estuary or arm of the sea.
Frem'd or *fremit*, far off, strange, or not near a-kin.
To *frist*, to trust for a time.
To *gang*, to walk.
To *garre*, to make.
A *garth*, a yard.
A *gilder*, a snare.
A *gimmer*, a ewe lamb.
To *greit* or *greet*, to cry.
A *haust*, or *host*, a dry cough.
To *lake*, to play.
Land, urine.
Lat, slow, lazy.
To *lear*, to learn.
A *poke*, a sack, or bag.
A *quie*, a heifer.

To *ram*, to reach.

A *fark*, a shirt.

Saur dirt, en faur pool, a stinking puddle.

To *fparre*, or *fpeir*, or *fpurre*, to ask, enquire.

Stark, stiff, strong.

To *thirl*, to drill, to bore a hole.

Walling, boiling.

Wang, the side.

From history, as well as from similarity of features, customs, and language, it is evident that the northern inhabitants of England, and of the lowland Scots, were originally the same people; being both descended from the nations on the shores of the Baltic; but chiefly from the Danes and the Norwegians: and the circumstance of their living now under the same government, cannot fail to restore their union, and to render it every day more and more complete.

It appears that, in former times, much emulation and great animosities prevailed between the people of England living on the south side of the river Trent, and those living on the north.* The famous Roger Aschem, who was preceptor to Queen Elizabeth, and was a North-Trentian, condescended to write a book to vindicate the dignity of the northern counties in England from the abuse of their southern neighbours. ---We are somewhat at a loss, at this day, to account for the disputes, and even the hostilities, that prevailed a few centuries ago, between the people on this side and beyond Trent. The time will come, when we will in like manner wonder at the animosities that still take place, in some degree, among the vulgar, on this side and beyond the Tweed.

That the people of England and Scotland may be still more effectually united, I would propose, that in all the sheriffs courts in Great Britain, trials should be determined by

---

* It is to the divided state of the country, in former times, that we are to trace the practice of appointing certain officers on this side and beyond Trent.

by juries: and that the Bishop of Durham should be the Diocesan of all the qualified Episcopalians in Scotland. It were also to be wished, that the Royal Burghs were restored to their original freedom of constitution, by which the inhabitants enjoyed, as they ought, the right of chusing their own magistrates, and demanding an account of the common revenue or estate. A Committee has been appointed by a great number of the Royal Burghs, for the purpose of urging their just claims at the tribunal of the nation, and the bar of the public, where there is not a doubt, if they proceed with the same temper, prudence, and perseverance which have hitherto marked their conduct, but they will meet with success. Farther still, it were to be wished, though not *yet* to be expected, that the right of voting in the election of representatives in parliament were extended, as in England, to all who possess freeholds of forty shillings annual rent.

rent. I say not *yet* to be expected, because, it is not improbable, that this may one day be effected by the progressive and mutual influence of industry, wealth, and a spirit of liberty, which may break entails, split aristocratical domains into a thousand pieces, and assert the rights of freemen. If this shall not be the case, the political importance of the people of Scotland, instead of being increased, must be diminished; for there is nothing human that is absolutely stationary. But there is a spirit in Scotland, at the present moment, that presages a brighter prospect, and which may repay to the sister kingdom, and that, perhaps, in a time of need, the generous fire which was kindled by her laws and examples.

At the same time that the Anglo-Saxons took possession of England, and the Scots of Caledonia, that is, the middle of the fifth century, the Franks, crossing the Rhine, established themselves in France, the Burgundians seized Burgundy, Savoy, and Dauphiné;

phinè; the Goths, that division of Old Gaul which was distinguished by the name of Aquitania; the Hunni, the rest of Gaul, Hungary, and other places; and the Vandals, Africa, Italy, and Rome itself. All these nations possessed, at that time, similar forms of government, and equal degrees of freedom. But, it is in Great Britain only, with the Low Countries, that any lively vestiges of the freedom, introduced by those barbarians, are now to be found. France, the freest of all European countries, maintained its civil liberties for a period of eleven hundred years; but at last sunk into slavery, the usual fate of nations, towards the end of the fifteenth century. These things naturally excite anxiety and alarm, nd teach a lesson of vigilance and circumspection.

If any of the foregoing observations may be deemed in any degree useful or instructive, it will be matter of great satisfaction to the Author, whose principal intention, in

taking

taking the liberty of publishing them, is, to induce men of learning and genius, of property and patriotic spirit, to visit a part of this island, which has hitherto been too much neglected, and where there is an ample field for improvement.

Expanded and cultivated minds may, by ocular demonstration, be convinced of the truth of this assertion: and while they are preserving health by exercise, and receiving pleasure from the beautiful and romantic scenery which will daily be presented to their view, they may derive the first of all gratifications, that of giving additional stability to the united kingdom of Great Britain, by promoting agriculture, encouraging its manufactories and fisheries, and, by emancipating a great part of the inhabitants of this island from sloth and idleness, make them active and useful members of society.

F I N I S.

www.ingramcontent.com/pod-product-compliance
Lightning Source LLC
Chambersburg PA
CBHW032020220426

43664CB00006B/316